The
WISDOM
of
SIKHISM

The

WISDOM

of

SIKHISM

Compiled by
Charanjit K. AjitSingh

O N E W O R L D

O X F O R D

THE WISDOM OF SIKHISM

Oneworld Publications
(Sales and Editorial)
185 Banbury Road
Oxford OX2 7AR
England
www.oneworld-publications.com

ISBN 1–85168–280–5

Cover and text design by Design Deluxe
Typeset by Cyclops Media Productions
Printed and bound by Graphicom Srl, Vicenza, Italy

CONTENTS

PREFACE

After making a commitment to writing on the wisdom of Sikhism and beginning to reflect on it, a strong self-doubt hit me. How can I, a mere follower, knowing so little of the deep ocean of the holy scriptures, full of golden nuggets and precious jewels, even attempt to undertake the task. I also had concerns about translating the passages from Gurmukhi to English and ensuring that the spirit and meaning of the original text is conveyed as far as possible – usually a daunting task when certain concepts, words and ideas do not render themselves to appropriate translation. Then the thought came into my mind that I needed to pray and ask permission of God to do it and to request God to help me do it; as the following hymn guides us:

> When you wish to perform a task
> Call upon God to assist
>
> God shall complete your work well,
> Is the testimony of the True Guru
>
> In the company of the holy
> Savour the precious Nectar

The Compassionate, Eradicator of fear
Will preserve the honour of the servant

Says Nanak, 'Sing the praises of the Lord
The Incomprehensible will become Comprehensible.'

GURU GRANTH SAHIB, p. 91

In deep gratitude to the divine, the work on this short anthology is accomplished. Hopefully, it conveys a few glimpses of the wisdom of the Sikh faith. The main Sikh scripture, Guru Granth Sahib, is the main source referred to; it is also known as Adi Granth among scholars to distinguish it from the Dasam Granth, the Tenth Guru Gobind Singh's composition, from which references are also drawn. To my mind the distinction is quite clear and the title Guru Granth Sahib reflects it. The last section of this book gives a flavour of the views of non-Sikh writers during the last two centuries. Compiling this anthology has been a great learning experience for me and a source of great inspiration: about God and the Sikh Gurus, about our responsibility to the divine, to the environment and to fellow beings as people of faith. May wisdom prevail. I would like to end this with the words spoken at the end of Sikh worship:

O God! Let your will prevail
May the whole creation benefit.

Charanjit Kaur AjitSingh

PICTURES

The editor and publisher would like to thank Ajit Singh for supplying the photographs used inside this book. Front cover image © Ilay Cooper/Images of India, 2001.

GOD

Mool Mantra in Sri Guru Arjan Dev's hand from Sri Kartarpuri Bir, the original of the Sikh holy scripture, Guru Granth Sahib.

ONE GOD

ONE GOD
Named Truth
Creator
Without fear
Without hate
Timeless, Immortal
Is neither born, nor dies
Self-existent
Is revealed by the grace of the Guru.
Truth in the beginning,
Truth through the ages
Truth now
Truth shall ever be.

JAPJI SAHIB, *first verse, The Mool Mantra*

FIRST, THE One God is unique
Immortal, unborn
Has no caste and is unattached
Beyond our approach
Beyond our comprehension
We searched and searched for God
Then found Him residing in our hearts.

GURU SAHIB, *p. 838*

O SUBLIME, Peerless and Boundless Lord!
Who can know your virtues?

Singers are saved,
Listeners are saved
And their countless sins dispelled.

You save the animals, the ghosts, demons
And the ignorant
And ferry them across the rocky oceans.

Your servant Nanak seeks your protection
And is forever a devotee of you.

GURU GRANTH SAHIB, *p. 802*

MY LORD is One
Is the One
My brother
The Lord is One.

GURU GRANTH SAHIB, *p. 350*

REMEMBER THE One
Praise the One
Pray to the One
Cherish the One
Sing adoration of the Infinite One
With body and mind meditate on the One
One God, One only, One God alone
The perfect God pervades all
Infinite creation flows from the One
Fears are cast away by worshipping the One
When body and mind are imbued with the One,
Says Nanak, by the grace of the Guru realise the One.

SUKHMANI SAHIB, *section 19, stanza 8*

ATTRIBUTES OF GOD

NO SHAPE, no outline and no colour
These three attributes make God distinct
God is revealed to those, says Nanak,
With whom God is happy.

SUKHMANI SAHIB, *verse 16*

NO CIRCLE, no mark, no colour, no caste, no family
How can one describe features, complexion, outline or
  clothes of God
Spoken of as eternal, self-illuminant and of Infinite
  power
Enumerated as the God of millions of deities
And as the King of Kings
Ruling emperor of the three worlds – gods, humans and
  demons –
Proclaimed everywhere as indescribable by low grasses
  and lofty forests
So who can recount all God's names?
The wise describe God by attributes and actions.

GURU GOBIND SINGH, *Jaap Sahib, verse 1*

I BOW IN reverence to the Immortal
I bow in reverence to the Compassionate
I bow in reverence to the Formless
I bow in reverence to the Incomparable

I bow in reverence to the Ungarbed
I bow in reverence to the Indescribable
I bow in reverence to the One without body
I bow in reverence to the Unborn

I bow in reverence to the Invincible
I bow in reverence to the Indestructible
I bow in reverence to the Nameless
I bow in reverence to the Placeless

I bow in reverence to God, who is beyond deeds
I bow in reverence to the One who is above formal observances
I bow in reverence to the One beyond names
I bow in reverence to the One beyond places

I bow in reverence to the Unconquerable
I bow in reverence to the Unafraid
I bow in reverence to the Unshakable
I bow in reverence to that which cannot be overthrown

I bow in reverence to the One who is without hue or
    shape
I bow in reverence to the One who is without beginning
I bow in reverence to the One who cannot be pierced
I bow in reverence to the One who is Unfathomable

I bow in reverence to the Unwinnable
I bow in reverence to the Unsmashable
I bow in reverence to the most Generous
I bow in reverence to the Boundless

I bow in reverence to the only One
I bow in reverence to the Countless
I bow in reverence to that beyond the five elements
I bow in reverence to that beyond entanglements

I bow in reverence to the One who is beyond action
I bow in reverence to the One who is beyond doubt
I bow in reverence to the One who is not confined to
countries or places
I bow in reverence to the One who is beyond camouflage

I bow in reverence to the Nameless
I bow in reverence to the Desireless
I bow in reverence to the Metaphysical
I bow in reverence to the Uninjurable

I bow in reverence to the Immovable
I bow in reverence to the One who is beyond natural
forces
I bow in reverence to the Invisible
I bow in reverence to the Sorrowless

I bow in reverence to the One who is beyond sickness
I bow in reverence to the One who cannot be installed
I bow in reverence to the One who is honoured in the
three worlds
I bow in reverence to the One True Treasure

I bow in reverence to the Unfathomable
I bow in reverence to the Self-Established
I bow in reverence to the Embodiment of three Supreme
    honours
I bow in reverence to the Uncreated

I bow in reverence to the Great Enjoyer
I bow in reverence to the All-Pervader
I bow in reverence to the Colourless
I bow in reverence to the Indestructible

I bow in reverence to the Inaccessible
I bow in reverence to the most Beautiful
I bow in reverence to the Sustainer of Oceans
I bow in reverence to the One who needs no help

I bow in reverence to the One who has no birth
I bow in reverence to the One who has no class
I bow in reverence to the One, the God of no religion
I bow in reverence to the Wondrous One

My salutation to the God of no land
I bow in reverence to the One who wears no robes
I bow in reverence to the One who has no dwelling
I bow in reverence to the One not born of a person

My salutation to the Annihilator of all
My salutation to the All Merciful
My salutation to the One permeating all life forms
My salutation to the Sovereign of all

My salutation to the Exterminator of all
My salutation to the Creator of all
My salutation to the Destroyer of all
My salutation to the Preserver of all

I bow in reverence to the Luminous, Worthy of Worship
I bow in reverence to the Mysterious
I bow in reverence to the Birthless
I bow in reverence to the Exquisite

My salutations to the One who reaches all
My salutations to the One who exists everywhere
My salutations to the Epitome of all colours
My salutations to the Remover of all

I salute the Destroyer of death
I salute the Symbol of kindness
I bow in reverence to the Indescribable who is above the
    prejudice of colour or race
I bow in reverence to the One who never dies

I bow in reverence to the Ageless
I bow in reverence to the Innovator
My salutation to the Action Maker
My salutation to the Freer of Bondage

I bow in reverence to the Kinless
I bow in reverence to the Fearless
I bow in reverence to the Benevolent
I bow in reverence to the Giver of Gifts

I bow in reverence to the Infinite
I bow in reverence to the Greatest
I bow in reverence to the God of Love
I bow in reverence to the most Fortunate

My salutations to the Ravager of all
My salutations to the Carer of all
My salutations to the Maker of all
My salutations to the Eradicator of all

My salutations to the Supreme Yogi
My salutations to the Supreme Reveller
My salutation to the Gracious to all
My salutations to the Nurturer of all

Formless, You are
Unparalleled, You are
Immovable, You are
Unborn, You are

Indescribable, You are
Un-costumed, You are
Nameless, You are
Wantless, You are

Inconceivable, You are
Mysterious, You are
Unconquerable, You are
Unafraid, You are

Worshipped in the three worlds, You are
Treasure of all, You are
Symbol of three ideals, You are
Never born, You are

Brilliant without colour, You are
Without beginning, You are
Invincible, You are
Primal Being, You are

No origin, You have
No race or colour, You have
Matterless, You are
Needless, You are

Undefeatable, You are
Uninjurable, You are
Unchallengeable, You are
Beyond controversy, You are

Very deep, You are
Friend of all, You are
Without entanglements, You are
Without fetters, You are

Enigmatic, You are
Baffling, You are
Timeless, You are
Unbonded, You are

Unattainable, You are
Placeless, You are
Boundless, You are
The Greatest, You are

Imageless, You are
Unrelated, You are
Non-dependent, You are
Non-understandable, You are

Unreachable, You are
Uncreated, You are
Not made of matter, You are
Untouchable, You are

Beyond our vision, You are
Away from worries, You are
Beyond our actions, You are
Free from doubt, You are

Unachievable, You are
Unfrightened, You are
Steady as a mountain, You are
Like a fathomless ocean, You are

Immeasurable, You are
Immensely invaluable, You are
Having countless forms, You are
Yet One, you are

DASAM GRANTH, *writings of the tenth Guru Gobind Singh,*
verses 1–43

GOD THE CREATOR

There is no one story of creation but many hymns containing references about creation in the Sikh holy book, which also contains reference to the Hindu Trinity – creator, preserver and destroyer – and scriptures and preachers of other world faiths.

GOD CREATED God's self
Created God's name
Second, created Nature,
Established self therein
And beholds it with joy.
You are the bountiful giver and Creator,
You give in plenty and you make the creation
You know all
You give life and take away life
With one word
You behold your creation with delight!

GURU NANAK, *Guru Granth Sahib*, p. 463

GOD SPOKE one word
And created the whole creation

JAPJI, *p. 1 – first reference*

THE FORMLESS created form

GURU GRANTH SAHIB, *p. 1065*

WHEN GOD created His own self
There was none other.
Took His own counsel and advice
What He did came to pass
Then there was no sky
No nether world, no three peoples
[Of heaven, earth and nether world]
Then there was only the Formless One
And nothing grew
As it pleased God, so God did
None other than Him.

GURU AMARDAS, *Guru Granth Sahib, p. 509*

FOR COUNTLESS ages there was foggy darkness
No earth, no sky,
Only the will of the Infinite.
No day or night, no moon or sun,
But God alone sat in deep meditation.
No realms, no sound
No air, no water.
No creation or destruction
No coming or going
No continents, no underworld
No seven oceans or flowing rivers.
Then no upper, middle or lower space
No hell or heaven
No death or time
No suffering or bliss
No birth or death
No one came and no one went.
There was no Brahma, or Vishnu or Shiva
None else but God seen.
No female or male
No caste or birth
No pain or pleasure.
Then there were no celibates
No people bound by vows, or doing penance in the forest.

No experts, no practitioners
And all lived in peace.
No yogis, no wandering monks
No religious uniforms
And none called himself Chief monk.
No prayer, no penance
No self-discipline, fasting or worship
None spoke or preached about another.
On creating His Own Self
God rejoiced and valued God's own worth.
There was no issue of purity
Nor self restraint
Nor rosary of Tulsi wood beads
No milk-maids nor Lord Krishna
No cows nor cowboys
No magic words nor spells
No hypocrite nor flute-player.
No karma, no religion
Nor the bee of mammon
Nor eyes could witness birth, race or caste.
No net of attachment cast
No death-time written on the forehead
Nor worship of any.
No blame, no seed, no soul nor life

Then no yogis like Gorakh or Machhinder.
Then no theology, no reflection,
No aristocracy, no growth
No sums, nor accounts.
No distinctions of race, colour or birth
Nor of styles of clothing or dress
Nor of high caste Brahmin or *Kshatri*.
No angels or gods, no worship places
Nor the cow, nor the key hymn of *Gayatri*.
No incense burning or feasting
No pilgrimages or dips in the sacred water
Nor the offering of prayer nor worship.
There was neither a mullah nor a judge
Nor a preacher, nor a penitent,
Nor a pilgrimage to Makka.
There was no subject, nor king
No ego, no world
Nor self promotion of great name.
No awe or wonder, no devotion
Neither mind, nor matter.
No friend, no lover
No seed, nor egg.
God, the only wealthy, the only merchant
Such was His wish!

No Vedas and other Hindu scriptures
No other books such as the Bible and the Qur'an
No readings of these scriptures
No dawn or dusk
God, the only speaker or preacher
Invisible self, yet saw everything.
When God so willed
God created the world,
Created the expanse of the sky without support.
Created Brahma, Vishnu and Mahesh
And developed the love of attachment.
Only the rare few are able to hear the Guru's word.
God has created, creates
And watches over the whole creation.
God founded the continents, solar systems, underworlds
From the invisible, God became manifest.
No one knows the extent of God,
This is the understanding obtained from the Guru.
Nanak says they rejoice and sing praises
Who are imbued with this truth of God.

GURU NANAK, *Guru Granth Sahib*, pp. 1035–6

FIRST GOD created light,
Nature and its beings
From the same light
The whole creation emerged

So who is good and who is bad
Never be in doubt, O people
God is in creation and creation is in God
God fulfils all spaces with His presence

Using the same mud,
The Creator has created
Many shapes in many ways
No fault in the pots made
As none in the Master Potter

The true one God is in all
By His doing is all done
A person who recognises the will of God
Is called the real human being

God being incomprehensible
Cannot be understood
But the Guru has given me
The sweet molasses of God's name

Kabir says: My doubt is removed
I recognise the Faultless Potter in all.

KABIR, *Guru Granth Sahib*, *p. 1349*

FROM THE divine command occurs the creation
And the dissolution of the universe

GURU GRANTH SAHIB, *p. 117*

GOD CREATED night and day
Seasons, time and occasions
So also are air, water, fire
And nether regions
Amidst these, He has fixed the earth
The place for Righteous Activities.

GURU GRANTH SAHIB, *p. 7*

DIVINE ORDER (HUKAM)

HOW CAN one be true?
How can the curtain of falsehood be torn?
By obeying the Divine Order
Says Nanak, as it is written:
By the Divine Order, all forms are created
But the Divine Order is beyond description
By the Divine Order, life is created
By the Divine Order, greatness is obtained
By the Divine Order, there are the high and the low
By the Divine Order, some suffer pain, others have joy
By the Divine Order, some are blessed, others trans-
    migrate
All are subject to the Divine Order, none outside it
Nanak, if the Divine Order is understood
Then 'I-am-ness' will be no more.

JAPJI SAHIB, *Guru Granth Sahib, p. 1*

AS IS the Divine Order,
So is their task.

JAPJI SAHIB, *Guru Granth Sahib, p. 8*

THE PRESENCE OF GOD

GOD IN water
God on land
God in hearts
God in nature

God in mountains
God in caves
God on earth
God in sky

God in here
God over there
God on the surface
God in the horizon

God is non-narrated
God is unclothed
God is without defects
God is without duality

God is beyond time
God is without a carer
God is indivisible
God is incomprehensible

God is not a conjuror
God is not a mantra
God is glorious
God is not a magician

God is without caste
God is without pedigree
God is without a friend
God is without a mother

God is without sickness
God is without grief
God is without doubt
God is above action

God is invincible
God is fearless
God is inscrutable
God is impenetrable

God is unbreakable
God is without criticism
God is without punishment
God is dazzling brilliant

God is the greatest
God is unfathomable
God needs no sustenance
God is indestructible

Remember God
Worship God
Meditate on God
Recite the word of God

You are in water
You are on land
You are in rivers
You are in the sea

You are in the trees
You are in the leaves
You are on Earth
You are in space

Sing Your Praises
Reflect on You
Dwell on You
Pray to You

You are the land
You are the sky
You are the owner
You are the house

You are free from incarnation
You are ever present
You are the way
You are everlasting

You are, You are
You are, You are
You are, You are
You are, You are

GURU GOBIND SINGH, *Akal Ustat*, *verses 51–70*

While on his travels westwards, Guru Nanak also visited Makka, the holiest shrine for the Muslims. On a hot summer evening, he arrived in the vicinity of the Kaaba and fell asleep there. He was rudely awoken by a furious imam who shouted at him, uttering, 'Wake up. Don't you know your feet are towards the house of God? How dare you show such disrespect?' The Guru answered politely, 'I am sorry for that. Please turn my feet towards where God is not.'

THE ENVIRONMENT AND GOD

NATURE WE see
Nature we hear
Nature we observe with awe, wonder and joy
Nature in the nether regions
Nature in the skies
Nature in the whole creation
Nature in the sacred texts (Vedas, Puranas and Qur'an)
Nature in all reflection
Nature in food, in water, in garments and in love for all
Nature in species, kinds, colours
Nature in life forms
Nature in good deeds
Nature in pride and in ego
Nature in air, water and fire
Nature in the soil of the earth
All nature is Yours, O powerful Creator
You command it, observe it and pervade it.

GURU GRANTH SAHIB, *p. 464*

THE FIRST living thing is water
Whereby each object is sustained

GURU GRANTH SAHIB, *p. 472*

REJOICE IN the Lord who dwells in nature

REHRAS, *Guru Granth Sahib, p. 469*

AIR IS the Guru
Water the father
Earth the great mother.
Day and night,
Male and female nurses
In whose lap the whole world plays.

JAPJI SAHIB, *Guru Granth Sahib, p.8*

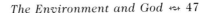

IF I WERE a doe living in the forest
Eating grass and leaves
With God's grace, I would find my groom
I would ever be a sacrifice to Him
I am the shopkeeper trading in God
Trading Your Name is my business
If I were a cuckoo living in the mango tree
Contemplating and singing the Word
God reveals through His mercy
Immense beauty and wonderful vision
If I were a fish living in water
Observing all the creatures therein
And my beloved lived on both sides of the water
I would hug Him with stretched arms
If I were a female snake dwelling in the ground
Let God's Word be in my being
My dread would vanish
Says Nanak, she is forever married
As light meets light

GURU GRANTH SAHIB, *p. 157*

501/-PARKASH KOUR W/o S. SWARN SINGH
BHATIA KRISHNA S.G. 54A. ASR

تاریخ ۵۵ء روپیے کی بیوا عاشبیر اُدوا بسٹر محمد عبداللہ پرانی دہلی
برای جُھوپینڈر رنگک انٹرنیشنے کرائی

HUMANS, TREES, holy places
Coasts, clouds, fields
Islands, continents, universes
Spheres and solar systems
Life forms – egg-born, womb-born, earth-born,
    sweatborn –
Only God knows their existence,
In oceans, mountains, everywhere
Nanak says, God created them
And God takes care of them all

JAPJI SAHIB

NATURE WORSHIPS GOD

IN THE round tray of sky
Are placed sun and moon as lamps,
And the spray of stars studded as pearls

The scent of sandalwood, the incense
The air gently moves to honour You
The whole vegetation
The offering of flowers

What a worship!
What a worship! O Remover of Fear!
The unplayed music of the Word sounds

Thousands of eyes are Yours, yet You have no eye
Thousands of images are Yours, yet You have no image
Thousands of feet are Yours, yet You have no feet
Thousands of noses are Yours, yet You have no nose
I am enthralled by Your amazing Creativity

There is light in all and it's the same light
With the same light we are all illuminated
The Guru's teachings reveal that light
Worship is what pleases You

My mind yearns as a bee for honey
Thirsty day and night to be with Your lotus-like feet
Nanak prays for your grace for a home in Your Name,
As the thirsty pied cuckoo bird for water

KEERTAN SOHILA, *second hymn*

RELATIONSHIP WITH GOD

I WAS A jobless minstrel
The Lord gave me work
Commanded me to sing
His praises, day and night
The Lord summoned the minstrel
To His Court of Truth
He awarded me with a robe
Of His True Honour and Praise
Then I was bestowed with the Nectar
The Nectar of His True Name
Those who savour this to their fill
At the Guru's instruction
Attain peace and happiness
The minstrel spreads Your Glory
By singing the Word
Nanak, through exalting the True Name
We attain the Most Perfect.

GURU GRANTH SAHIB, *p. 150*

The hymn on the preceding page describes how Guru Nanak received instructions from God to preach His message. It is said that one day, Nanak as usual went for an early morning dip in the river Weyin, the way it was customary to do ablutions, but he did not return. His clothes were later found on the river bank and the people of the town of Sultanpur thought that he had drowned in the river. The river was searched by divers and nets were cast but no body was found and his family resigned themselves to the loss. To their surprise, Nanak appeared from the river after three days and stayed quiet. Eventually he spoke in a sort of a riddle: 'Neither Hindu, nor Muslim.' These words are interpreted in a number of ways and are applicable in our multi-religious world:

🌱God is neither Hindu nor Muslim, these are the labels and God is above human labels. Therefore, we should follow the path to God rather then be stuck with the label of being a Hindu, Muslim, Buddhist, Christian or Jew.

🌱We are all one humanity, children of the same Creator. We share a universal heritage and we should aim to be part of that humanity and work towards it regardless of our religious and other backgrounds.

Neither Hindus nor Muslims are practising their religion in the way they were taught by their prophets. They need to study the essence of their religion and act upon it in their everyday lives. There are many hymns in Guru Granth Sahib about what it is to be a person of faith in those religions. (Hinduism and Islam were the two main religions in India at the time of Guru Nanak).

Guru Nanak then explained to those present that he was taken to the court of God, where God gave him a cup of amrit (nectar) to drink and told him, 'I have sent you to the world to spiritually liberate suffering humanity. Instruct them in meditating and singing glories of the True Name, so that they gain the right to salvation; this includes those that do evil. Let this be your work.' Guru Nanak humbly accepted the task and began his mission.

NOW I relate my story
How I was brought here from my deep meditation
Where the mountain known as Hemkunt is
Adorned by the crown of seven summits
Which are named Saptsring
Pandava rulers did penance there

There I performed intense meditation
There I prayed to the Timeless and Immortal Being
Thus I continued until I became one with the Divine
My parents also prayed to the Incomprehensible
They meditated upon and worshipped God in many ways
They served the Indescribable with such devotion
That God became much pleased with them
When God commanded me
Then I took birth in this dark age.
My mind did not wish to come
As my concentration was in the feet of God
God in many ways made me understand
And directed me into this world

'I call you as my son
Have created you to show the right path,
Spread righteousness everywhere
And stop people from doing evil deeds.'
I stood there with bowed head and folded hands
And I prayed, 'Righteousness can only spread with Your
    Grace.'
It was for this reason that God sent me
Then I took birth in this world
As He told me, so shall I do, to say

I have no enmity towards anyone
Those who would call me God
Shall fall into the depth of hell
Regard me as the servant of Him
Do not ever doubt it
I am a menial slave of the Supreme Being
I have come into the world to witness its play
What the Lord told me, I convey to all
And I will not be silenced by the mortals of this earth.

For this purpose, I came into this world
The Supreme Guru has sent me to protect righteousness
Was told to spread righteousness everywhere
And destroy the wicked and evil
I have taken birth for this reason
O saints and holy people! understand it well
I have come to spread the divine faith
And to uproot the evil sinners.

GURU GOBIND SINGH, *Bachitra Natak, verses 29–43*

ONE GOD is my friend
One God is my love
One God is my soul-mate
One God is my companion.
With one God I converse
Who does not turn away
Or show anger
Knows my innermost feelings
And never jolts love.
God alone is my counsel
Omnipotent; creates, destroys, recreates.
God alone is the provider
Who protects by placing a hand on those
Who contribute in the world.
God alone is my protector
Who is all-powerful
Above the heads of all.
The saint, true Guru
Put his hand upon my forehead
And enabled me to meet God.
The Guru helped me to meet the Great God
Who has saved the whole world.
My wishes are fulfilled
And I am united as predestined, with God

Nanak says, whoever finds the True Name,
Forever enjoys God's feast.

GURU ARJAN, *Guru Granth Sahib*, p. 958

YOU ARE my father
You are my mother
You are my kin
You are my brother
You are my Saviour everywhere
Why should I fear, why should I worry?

Through your grace
I recognise you
You are my shelter
You are my pride
None other except you
All around is your playground
All beings, big and small, are your creation
They work under your will
All that is done is your doing
Nothing is ours

Meditating on your Name
I achieved tremendous happiness
Singing your praises, O God
My mind is at peace
By the grace of the perfect Guru
Congratulations, felicitations!
Nanak says; discord has been won over.

GURU ARJAN, *Rag Majh, p. 103*

YOU ARE the Lord, to you we pray
Body and soul are your gifts to us
You are the mother and father
We are your children
In your grace lies abundant peace
Your bounds are beyond us
You are higher than the highest
The whole creation is threaded together through you
And abides in your Will
You alone know your mystery
Nanak, your servant, is forever your sacrifice.

GURU GRANTH SAHIB, *Sukhmani Sahib, p. 268*

TRUST IN GOD

O MY MIND, why are you worried about your needs?
As God is involved
God has created life in rocks and stones
And sustains them

O human, you get in the company
Of the people of faith to be saved.
By the grace of God
Even dead wood becomes green

Neither mother, nor father, nor others
Nor son, nor wife supports anyone
God sends sustenance for everyone
Then why should you be concerned?

Flamingos fly hundreds of miles
And leave their young behind
Who feeds them and teaches them how to feed?
They worship God in their hearts

In the palms of God's hands
Lie all treasures and powers
Nanak, the servant, says

'O God, I am forever dedicated to You
Whose benevolence is limitless.'

GURU ARJAN, *Rehras, Sacred Nitnem, p. 218*

THROUGH PRAYER and meditation to the perfect Lord
My tasks are successful
The Creator lives in the Creator town
With saints

There is no obstacle
When you pray to the Guru
God, the master Saviour
Protects the devotees' treasures (inner and outer)

No shortage ever and the treasury full
My mind and body are blessed
As the home of the lotus feet of God
My Lord who is inaccessible and infinite

Those who are in the service of God
Are at peace and see no shortage.
By the blessings of the saints
Meet God, the Ultimate Lord of the World.

Congratulations, congratulations!
All say, Magnificent is the True One's place.
Nanak meditates on the Lord,
Gains perfect peace
And receives the perfect Guru.

GURU GRANTH SAHIB, *pp. 816–7*

GOD'S GRACE

'ONE GOD, obtained through Guru's grace'.

*These words occur at the start of many verses in the holy
scripture.*

> BY WHOSE grace you enjoy thirty-six heavenly foods
> Have that Lord always in mind
> By whose grace, you put perfume on your body
> By meditating on Him
> You shall gain ultimate salvation
> By whose grace, you live in peace in beautiful homes
> Concentrate on Him in your heart
> By whose grace, you live in happiness at home
> Throughout the hours, utter His Name with your tongue
> By whose grace, you engage in pleasures
> Always reflect on the One worthy of reflection, says
> Nanak.
>
> By whose grace, you wear silks and satins
> Why forsake that One and want another?

By whose grace, you sleep in peace in bed
O mind, Sing His praises day and night
By whose grace, you are honoured by all
Sing and talk about His glory
By whose grace, your commitment is maintained
O mind, meditate ever on the one Supreme Being
By concentrating on Beloved God, you shall be honoured
  in the Divine Court
Nanak says: 'You will return to your heavenly home with
  grace.'

By whose grace, you have a beautiful and healthy body
Be attached to that loving God
By whose grace, your sins are overlooked
O mind, find peace through adoration of God
By whose grace, your mistakes stay hidden
O mind seek shelter of that Lord
By whose grace, none can reach your level
Remember that highest Lord with every breath
By whose grace, you received the precious human body
Nanak, be a devotee of That Lord

By whose grace, you adorn yourself with jewels
O mind, why do you get too lazy to worship Him
By whose grace, you ride horses and elephants

O mind, never forget that God
By whose grace, you have garden, property, wealth
O mind, thread as pearls, the priceless Lord within you
That which shaped your mind and body
Sitting and standing, you must remember Him
Meditate on the One who is Incomprehensible
Nanak, who protects you here and the hereafter

By whose grace, you perform many charitable acts
Remember that One all hours
By whose grace, you perform religious and secular duties
Remember that Lord with every breath
By whose grace, you have beauty
Remember always the Most Beautiful
By whose grace, you received noble birth
Remember that God every day and night
By whose grace, your dignity is protected
With Guru's grace, Nanak, say His praises

By whose grace, you hear the holy music with your ears
By whose grace, you behold breathtaking wonder
By whose grace, you speak sweetly with your tongue
By whose grace, you live happily in comfort
By whose grace, your hands move and work
By whose grace, you gain full fruition

By whose grace, obtain the highest bliss
By whose grace, attain peace and equanimity
Why abandon such God and follow another?
With Guru's grace, Nanak, awaken your mind
With whose grace, you emerge in the world
Never ever forsake that Lord from your heart
By whose grace, you receive fame
O foolish mind, meditate upon Him
By whose grace, your work is perfected
O mind, consider that Ever-present and near
By whose grace, you find the Truth
O my mind, you be immersed in That
By whose grace, all are saved
Nanak, practise that Name with all your effort.

Whom God graces, recites His name
Whom God causes to sing, sings praises of the Lord
With God's blessing, divine light dawns
With God's compassion, the heart blossoms as a water
    lily
When God is pleased, then He resides in the mind
When God is benevolent, sublime wisdom is attained

With your mercy, O God! All wealth is obtained
None can achieve on one's own
O God, our master, where you put us, that we do
Nanak, our hands on their own have nothing.

GURU ARJAN, *Sukhmani Sahib, Guru Granth Sahib*, pp.
269–70

OUR ACTIONS determine our birth
God's grace determines our liberation

JAPJI, *verse 4, Guru Granth Sahib*, p. 2

BONDAGE AND liberation are through grace
By the grace of the Guru
One is emancipated

GURU GRANTH SAHIB, *p. 1011*

WHERE THE lowly, the poor, are looked after
There is your grace
There is your blessing

GURU GRANTH SAHIB, *p. 15*

WE ARE rid of desire through the Guru's grace.

GURU GRANTH SAHIB, *p. 1320*

THOSE ON whom God casts a glance of grace
Nanak, are immersed in the joy of that grace

JAPJI, *verse 38*

LOVE OF GOD, LOVE OF THE GURU

WHAT IS this love
Which is for another?
Nanak, a lover is really one
Who ever remains merged in the Divine.
A lover is not the one
Who is happy only in happy times
And miserable in adversity
A lover is not the one
Who only wants to barter the love of God for his own gain

GURU ANGAD, *Guru Granth Sahib*, p. 474

O MY BELOVED! You gave me the garment of Your Love
To cover my honour
My Master, You are wise and accomplished
I realise not Your worth

GURU GRANTH SAHIB, *p. 520*

WITH THE love of God eternal peace is attained
With the love God there is no suffering
With the love of God the dirt of self-centredness is
    removed
With the love of God the immaculate state is achieved
    forever
My friend, cultivate such love for God
Who is the sustainer of every life and every heart
With the love of God all treasures are received
With the love of God the pure name enters the mind
With the love of God fame is bestowed
With the love of God stress anxiety is removed
With the love of God the ocean of death is crossed
With the love of God the messenger of hell stays away
With the love of God all are saved
The love of God continues with the mortal after death
By self alone one neither finds God nor forgets ego
The one to whom God shows grace
Joins the congregation of the righteous
Nanak says, 'O God I am a sacrifice to you
As you are the shelter and strength of saints.'

GURU GRANTH SAHIB, *p. 391*

Love of God, Love of the Guru 73

GOD'S CHAMPION

I AM THE small wrestler of the Master of the World
Having met the Guru I have begun wearing a turban with
   high plume.

All have gathered to witness the wrestling,
The Compassionate Lord is seated to watch it too.

The accordions, drums and trumpets are playing,
The strong wrestlers enter the stadium and
   circumambulate it.

I have thrown the five strong young men*
The Guru gave me a big pat on my back.

All have come together
They shall go back home by different ways.

The devotees of the Guru take their gains with them
While the selfish individuals leave losing even their
   capital.

* Symbols of evil passions – lust, anger, greed, worldly attachment,
ego/arrogance.

O God, You are outside the realm of colour or mark,
Yet You are clearly present everywhere.

Hearing your praises, Your devotees recite them
O, the Fount of Excellent Qualities.

I am the female servant of God in every age
The Guru has cut my shackles.

I will never again perform the wrestling dance
Nanak has found this timely opportunity after a lot of
    searching.

GURU ARJAN, *Guru Granth Sahib, p. 74*

FOUR CASTES and their religious experts,
Who have the six systems of Hindu philosophy in the
    palms of their hands,

The handsome, the clever, the wise are all cheated by the
    five evil warriors
Who is such a courageous person who eradicates these
    five warriors?

The only complete being is the one in this dark age
Who has vanquished and destroyed these five.

Theirs is a great nation, fully disciplined, and does not
   run away
As their army is committed and topmost
Nanak says, 'That person will never be crushed
Who has the protective company of the holy people.'

GURU ARJAN, *Guru Granth Sahib*, *p. 404*

THE BATTLE drum beat in the sky
And the aimed arrow
Inflicted the wound.

The real warriors
Enter the battlefield
And are ready to fight.

That person alone is the warrior
Who fights for the faith,
Dies by being cut digit by digit
And never leaves the field.

GURU GRANTH SAHIB, *p. 1105*

HUMAN LIFE

THE VALUE OF HUMAN BIRTH

AMONG THE eight million and four hundred thousand life
    forms
The Supreme form is to be born with the human body
Eyes to see, ears to listen, mouth to speak endearing
    words
Hands to work with and feet to walk to meet together in
    the congregation
To earn a good honest living and to value sharing that
    with others.
Guruward beings make their own lives worthwhile,
By reading, understanding and listening to the scriptures,
Help fellow worshippers to be happy
By putting the Guru's sacred water into their mouths,
Do not stop bowing to the feet
In this age of darkness, praise God
Such disciples find salvation and help others to do so.

BHAI GURDAS, *Var 1, Pauri 3*

KABIR SAYS, human birth is very rare
It does not happen again and again:
As a fruit of a tree falls to the ground
And is not again attached to the same branch.

KABIR, *Guru Granth Sahib, p. 1366*

YOU HAVE received the human body
Your opportunity to meet God, the Preserver.

Your other tasks are of no value
But to be with holy people and recite only the Name.

Prepare to cross the fearful world ocean
Your life is being wasted in physical pleasures.

You have not practised praying,
Meditating, self-control and righteousness,
Did not serve the holy people or recognise the Sovereign
   God.

Nanak says, 'Our deeds are unworthy
We seek your shelter; save our honour, O God.'

GURU ARJAN, *Guru Granth Sahib, p. 12*

The Value of Human Birth ❧ 79

[HUMANKIND] ATTAINED human body
Through immense good fortune

Those who do not meditate on God
Do the same as those who commit suicide.

Why don't they die who neglect the Ever Present God
What is life worth without remembering God?

Eating, drinking, playing, laughing and being pretentious
Of what use is the beautification of the dead?

Those who do not hear praise of the Lord of Supreme
   Bliss
Are worse than animals, birds and insects.

Nanak says, 'The Guru has helped me practise
The mantra of Name
The Name alone is embedded in my mind.'

GURU GRANTH SAHIB, *p. 155*

TAKE CARE of your priceless body
So that you do not cut a sorry figure in God's court.

May you be honoured
In this and the next world
May God deliver you at the last moment of your life.

Sing God's praises
Meditate on the Wondrous Lord
So that life here and hereafter stays beautiful.

Reflect on the Lord,
Sitting and standing
So that all your troubles vanish.

May all your enemies become friends
And your mind become pure
This is the highest action.

Of all faiths it is the highest faith,
By meditating on God
You attain salvation
And are rid of the burden of sins of numerous past lives.
May your wishes be granted
And the noose of death be cut.

GURU ARJAN, *Guru Granth Sahib*, p. 895

LIVING A successful life,
Hearing God's praises,
Reciting God's praise,
Living forever.

Drink that drink which satisfies the mind
The nectar of immortality.

Eat such food as never to be hungry again,
Always content, always full.

Wear that which protects honour before God
Not to be naked again.

Soak in the mind such pleasure of the joy of God
Engrossed in the company of the holy people.

To sew the mind with God's devotion,
Without needle and thread.

Intoxicated with the nectar of God
One would never face problems.

One to whom the kind God gives
Is blessed with all the bounty.

Peace is in the service of the holy people
Wash their feet and drink the holy water.

GURU ARJAN, *Guru Granth Sahib*, p. 1018–9

BY SERVING the Guru and practising devotion
The human body is attained.

The angels pray for this body
For God can only be served by this body.

Worship God of the world
Do not forget
This alone is the benefit of the human life form.

So long as the sickness of old age has not come
So long as death has not grasped the body

So long as the speech has not become slurred
Till then you pray to the Lord of the World.

O brother, if you don't meditate now
When will you?
When the end comes
You won't be able to.

What you need to do,
Now is the most opportune time for it
Otherwise you will repent
When you can't get across.

A servant is the one
Whom God has put to serve
That person attains the Immaculate Master.

Having met the Guru
Doors of wisdom are opened
And that being is saved from the circle of life and death.

This is your chance
This is your turn
Look into your mind
Reflect on it.

Kabir says, 'It's up to you
Whether you win or lose
You have been told this aloud
Again and again.'

KABIR, *Guru Granth Sahib*, p. 1159

The Value of Human Birth 87

HUMAN RESPONSIBILITY TOWARDS THE DIVINE

IN MANY lives, became insects and moths
In many lives, became elephant, fish and deer
In many lives, became bird and snake
In many lives, became yoked horse and ox
This is your turn to meet God, the Lord of All
This human body has been shaped after a long wait

GURU ARJAN, *Guru Granth Sahib*, *p. 176*

O MY mind, you are the embodiment of God's light
Remember your root!

GURU GRANTH SAHIB, *p. 441*

O MY body, God installed the light in you
That is why you came into the world.

GURU AMARDAS, *Guru Granth Sahib*, *p. 921*

YOU HAVE been blessed with the human body
Our time to meet the Divine Sovereign
All other tasks are of no value,
Except to join the Society of spiritual people
And meditate.
Be prepared to swim across the tortuous world ocean
You are wasting your life in worldly pleasures
Have not practised meditation, self-discipline and
    responsibility,
Not been of service, nor served holy people, nor
    recognised the divine.
Nanak says, 'My deeds are mean, O God!
I seek your shelter, Save my honour.'

GURU ARJAN, *Guru Granth Sahib*, p. 12

HUMAN RELATIONSHIPS

TO YOU the Lord we pray.
Soul and body are your gifts to us.
You are the Mother, and the Father,
We are your children,
With your grace,
There are countless blessings.

GURU ARJAN, *Sukhmani Sahib*

The Elevation of Women

BORN OF a woman
Conceived in a woman
Demand marriage with a woman
You seek the friendship of a woman
Continue future life through a woman
When one woman dies
Seek another one

Why call her evil
Through whom sovereigns are born?

GURU GRANTH SAHIB, p. 473

Guru Nanak was challenged by some ascetics at a festival because he was leading a family life. He was asked, 'Why do you, a religious preacher, add sour rennet to milk by leading a married life?' He replied, 'You have not achieved what you preach. If you had why would you go begging for food to the women whom you denounce?'

When Babar, who later became the first Mughal ruler of India, invaded Punjab in North-West India in 1521 and his army visited atrocities upon people in general and women in particular, Guru Nanak described the women's condition in the following verse:

THOSE WHOSE heads were adorned with fashionable hair styles
And the parting of their hair decorated with vermilion
Are subjected to the humiliation of a forced hair cut
And there is dust around their necks.

As a result he made a strong complaint to God:

> THEY WERE tortured and writhing in agony
> Did you not suffer pain, O God?

Mata Khivi, the wife of the second Guru Angad, is immortalised in Guru Granth Sahib thus:

> MATA KHIVI IS the embodiment of goodness
> She is like a big shady tree full of leaves
> On a hot summer day.
> She distributes the treasure of sacred food
> Sweet, heavenly, butter-rich rice pudding.
> The faces of the disciples are radiant
> And the selfish turn as pale as straw
> Her masterly performance is accepted by the Divine
> Guru.

GURU GRANTH SAHIB, *p. 967*

Marriage

O YOUNG woman, if you wish to find a groom
Concentrate on the Guru's feet
Then you shall forever be a happy bride of the Lord
Who neither dies nor leaves.

The Great God does not die or go;
With the Guru's calm temperament
The bride becomes the beloved of the groom.

Through the practice of truth and self-discipline
She becomes pure
And her decoration is the Guru's word.

My beloved Lord is true,
Is forever true
Who created His own self.

Nanak, she is imbued with love of her husband
Whose mind remains on the feet of the Guru.

When the youthful bride receives her husband
She remains intoxicated with his love day and night.

With the teaching of the Guru
She feels bliss
No impurity stays in her body.

No impurity in her body
She is full of love of the Sovereign God
My Lord causes the union.

GURU AMARDAS, Guru Granth Sahib, p. 771

COME SISTERS, come friends
Let's hug each other
Let's talk about the stories of our Omnipotent Divine
    Husband.

The True Master has all the divine strengths
We have all the weaknesses.

O Creator, You have the power over all
I reflect on the One Word

If you are with me
What else do I want?
Go and ask the happy wives
What qualities they have
To receive love from their husbands.

They say that their ornaments are
Wisdom, contentment and sweet language,
You meet the Loving Supreme Husband
By following the Guru's advice.

GURU GRANTH SAHIB, *pp. 17–18*

RESPECTFULLY O Nanak,
I have given up praise and blame
I have given up 'I-am-ness'
I have found all my relations as bitter
Then I got myself attached to you.

GURU GRANTH SAHIB, *p. 963*

The Sikhs are shown the way to a truly spiritual marriage, in these words:

> THEY ARE not husband and wife,
> Who merely stay together,
> They are,
> Who have one light in two bodies.

GURU GRANTH SAHIB, *p. 788*

As shown in the verse below, men are told that they should consider other women as their mothers, daughters and sisters and not as mere sex objects to be exploited.

> WHEN YOU see women unrelated to you
> Consider them as good
> And as mothers, daughters and sisters.

BHAI GURDAS, *Var 29, Pauri 11*

> I ADORE the man who does not go to some other woman.

BHAI GURDAS, *Var 12, Pauri 4*

BE CHASTE with one woman, consider the other as sister or daughter.

BHAI GURDAS, *Var 6, Pauri 8*

INCREASE YOUR love for your wife every day
Not even in your dreams think of another.

GURU GOBIND SINGH

MAY YOUR eyes not see the other woman's beauty

GURU ARJAN-SUKHMANI, *Guru Granth Sahib, p. 274*

MEN AND women should be faithful in marriage and love and respect each other.

Sikh code of conduct

Mother's blessing

WORSHIP THE One who removes all sins
And liberate the ancestors
Ever pray to that Perfect God
Who has no end nor any limit.
O my son! Your mother gives you this blessing
May you never forget God
May God never forget you
May you always remember the Lord of the World
May the true Guru be kind to you
May you love the company of the holy
May your garments be your honour saved by God
And singing God's praises your daily food
May you drink the nectar of immortality
May you live long
May you remain in bliss forever in prayer to God
May you be blessed with joy and pleasure
May your desires be fulfilled
May you never be anxious
May your mind be a humming-bee at the lotus feet of God
Says Nanak, the servant, 'Attach yourself to them
As the cuckoo blossoms with joyful song with raindrops.'

GURU GRANTH SAHIB, *p. 496*

RESPECT FOR LIFE AND NON-VIOLENCE

AS THE mother gives birth to a son,
Keeps a constant watch over him
And brings him up,
At home and outside feeds him
With nourishing food
And loves him every moment.
In the same way, the true Guru
Cares for his follower
With deep love.

GURU GRANTH SAHIB, *p. 168*

THE AGE is knife
The kings are butchers
Religion has taken wings
And flown in the dark night of falsehood
The rise of the moon of truth
Is nowhere to be seen.

GURU NANAK, *Guru Granth Sahib, p. 145*

THOSE WHO beat you with fists, do not give them blows
Go to their homes yourself and kiss their feet.

BABA FARID, *Guru Granth Sahib, p. 1378*

NEVER SAY that the Vedas, Qur'an and other holy books
  are false
False is the one who does not reflect on them.
If you say that there is God in every being,
Then why kill a chicken?

KABIR, *Guru Granth Sahib, p. 1350*

COUNTLESS COMMIT sin by beheading.

JAPJI SAHIB, *verse 18*

When Ajita Randhawa asked Guru Nanak about ahimsa *(non-violence), Nanak replied:*

- DO NOT wish evil for anyone. This is *ahimsa* of thought.

- Do not speak harshly of anyone. This is *ahimsa* of speech.

- Do not obstruct anyone's work. This is *ahimsa* of action

- If a man speaks ill of you, forgive him.

- Practise physical, mental and spiritual endurance.

- Help the suffering even at the cost of your life.

RADHAKRISHNAN, *Sacred Writings of the Sikhs, p. 22*

When Guru Arjan, the fifth Guru, was tortured in a number of gruesome ways, he remained peaceful and utterly non-violent and accepted it as the will of God. His words were:

EVERY DAY meditate on the Name of God
And bring liberation for friends and companions too
My Guru is with me always
Pray and pray to the One who ever protects.
What You do, I find as sweet,
Nanak begs for the Divine Name.

GURU GRANTH SAHIB, *p. 394*

FEAR NOT, frighten not

GURU TEGH BAHADUR

WHEN ALL other efforts fail
It is right to take up the sword

GURU GOBIND SINGH-ZAFARNAMA

HUMILITY

THE SIMBAL tree is straight like an arrow
And extremely tall and thick
Those birds that come with hope
Leave disappointed.

Its fruit is tasteless, its flowers sickening
And its leaves are of no use
O Nanak: sweetness is low
And has much goodness and virtue.

Everyone bows for self
No one bows for the other
If you weigh with a balance
The lower side is the heavier.

The sinner bows double,
Such as the hunter who kills deer,
What good is the bowing of one's head
If your mind is wandering somewhere else?

GURU NANAK, *Guru Granth Sahib, p. 470*

HUMILITY IS our mace with spikes
To be the dust under everybody's feet
Is my double-edged sword
No evil-doer dare withstand these weapons
The Perfect Guru has made this possible
God's Name is the saints' refuge
Whoever reflects on it is liberated
Millions are freed thereby.
In the gathering of the holy
God's praises are sung
And the Perfect divine treasure is obtained.
Says Nanak, 'By effacing self–centredness
See the Transcendent all around.'

GURU GRANTH SAHIB, *p. 628*

KABIR SAYS, 'I am the worst of all
Leaving me aside, all are good.
Whoever understands this
Is my friend.'

GURU GRANTH SAHIB, *p. 1364*

THE TREE that looks downwards to earth
Is blessed with thousands of delicious fruit.

Only that water is deemed to be pure
That flows downwards.

One's head is high and feet are low
But the head of the follower
Bows humbly low to the Guru's feet.

The lowliest of the lowly is the earth
From whom the whole world gets food and wealth.

That land is very special, that place is very special
Where the Guru, the disciple, the holy person put their
    feet.

The value of such dust touched by the holy feet
Is sung by the Vedas and saints
Those are the fortunate ones
Whose foreheads receive that sacred dust.

BHAI GURDAS, *Var 26, verse 15*

KABIR, BE like a pebble on a path
Lay aside your own pride
If you become such a lowly servant
Then you will meet the Magnificent Lord

But what is the use of a pebble
For it would hurt a walker
Your servant should be such, God
As the dust on land

Kabir, what then of the dust
Which moves with wind and covers the body?
God's servant should be like the water
Which cleanses all parts of the body

Kabir, what then of the water
Which becomes hot or cold
God's being should be
Such as God is.

GURU GRANTH SAHIB, *p. 1372*

GOD IS like sugar
Dropped in the sand
Difficult for an elephant to pick up.
Kabir says, 'The Guru enabled me
To understand this great mystery:
Only an ant can eat it.'

GURU GRANTH SAHIB, *p. 1377*

HONEST EARNING AND OTHER KEY PRINCIPLES

ONE WHO lives by earning through hard work,
Then gives some of it away in charity,
Knows the way to God.

GURU GRANTH SAHIB, *p. 1245*

Bhumia the thief's conversion

A farmer named Bhumia lived in Dhaka. He lived by robbing travellers during the day and burgling people's homes at night. He had told people in his town that if a holy person, a sadhu, came that way, he was not to be allowed to stay the night in town with them or Bhumia would take away all they owned by force.

They asked Bhumia, 'If pilgrims ask to stay, what should we say?'

Bhumia replied, 'Send them to my house.'

To look after the pilgrims, Bhumia built an inn in his courtyard and food was made available there day and night. Whosoever came was not allowed to leave without eating there. On his travels with his companions Bala and Mardana, Guru Nanak stopped in the town close to the house of a gentleman. Many people gathered round and paid their respects to the Guru. They requested him not to stay there, since Bhumia, the headman of the area had commanded them to send any visiting holy person or pilgrim to his house.

The Guru accepted their request and said to Bala and Mardana, 'Let's go and stop at Bhumia's place.'

When Bhumia heard the news that three spiritual people had come to his place, he went to see them where they were sitting and prostrated himself in front of the Guru.

The Guru blessed him with, 'May God give you goodness.'

Then Bhumia folded his hands and begged the Guru and his companions, 'The food is ready, please give me the honour of serving you.'

The Guru replied gently, 'We shall have our meals in a while,' knowing full well what was in the mind of Bhumia. 'You serve food day and night. Tell us, how do you earn a living to keep this service going?'

Bhumia was so much influenced by the Guru's personality and his way of addressing him that he came out truthfully with what he actually did to raise money.

He said, 'O Compassionate and Caring Guru, my work is to rob the wayfarers during the day and burgle at night.'

When he expressed that, the Guru responded, 'O brother, we cannot partake of such a meal.'

Bhumia then beseeched them, 'If you don't put anything from here in your mouth, how will good happen to me?'

The Guru replied, 'O brother, when you stop robbery and theft and begin earning your living by honest means, then we will eat at your place. God gives to everybody and also to you when you work hard with honesty.'

Bhumia expressed his inability to change, saying, 'This is my family's trade. My father and my grandfather did this work. How can I leave this work?'

The Guru addressed those gathered around him, 'Bhumia has told the truth. This truth is the husband of all, only those on whom God casts His grace have it.'

He then put a condition to Bhumia, 'We will take the meal here if you promise to adhere to three things.'

Bhumia was delighted at this and answered quickly, 'I will do what you want me to do except that which I mentioned I can't do.'

The Guru then said, 'O dear disciple, listen carefully. First you must always speak the truth. Second, do not do any bad deed to the household from which you have tasted salt. Third, do not let the poor suffer.'

Bhumia prostrated himself in front of the Guru as a mark of acceptance. Then Guru Nanak recited his composition on the value of truth. It is:

> YOU ARE the One true Master
> Who has spread truth in a true manner
> To whom you give, they receive the truth
> And they practice it and live by it
> With meeting the True Guru, Truth is obtained
> Who caused the truth to be embedded in the heart.
> The foolish don't know the truth,
> The selfish, self-centred lose the precious life
> Why came they into this world?

GURU GRANTH SAHIB, *p. 467*

Guru Nanak reiterated to Bhumia that truth is accepted in God's presence, and observing a code of conduct. Bhumia wished to know what that code is. Guru Nanak expressed it in the following verse:

> TRUE IS known the one who has truth in the heart
> The dirt of falsehood comes off and the body becomes
>   clean.
> True is known the one who has deep love of Truth

Whose heart blossoms at hearing the Word Name
And enters the door of liberation.
True is known the one who knows how to live
Who prepares his body as a bed of earth
And sows the seed of the Creator God.
True is known the one who receives the true learning
Shows kindness to all living beings and gives in charity
True is known the one who resides in the holy place of
soul
Gets instruction from the Guru and stays and lives by
that.
Truth is the remedy for all and it washes away all sins
Nanak entreats those who have the wrap of Truth.

Guru Granth Sahib, *p. 468*

After listening to these verses in Guru Nanak's melodious voice, Bhumia nodded his head, uttering 'O holy saint! I obey your commands and I promise that I will observe them.'

The Guru pardoned all his previous and present evil deeds and made it clear to him that he would be the witness to Bhumia's actions in God's court provided he met the three conditions. On Bhumia's promise of acceptance, Guru Nanak and his companions accepted his hospitality, shared his food and stayed with him for five days. After they had gone, Bhumia began to reflect on the time spent with the Guru and his own way of life. How lucky he felt to receive such holy company but how could he fulfill his own needs? He thought up a plan. Rather than looting the visitors and stealing from ordinary people, he decided to burgle a royal household. That way he would get more wealth and jewellery, which would sustain him and his food service to travellers for a long time.

After showering himself, he dressed well with high quality clothes, a special turban and gold and diamond jewellery and late at night went to the palace. A doorman stopped him and asked, 'Who are you at this late hour wanting to go into the palace?'

Bhumia replied truthfully, 'I'm a thief', the promise to the Guru to speak the truth ringing in his ears while also he worried that he might be killed by the King's men. The doormen did not believe him at all. One of them said, 'You seem to be one of us. You're jesting.' The other said, 'If he were a thief, how could he say that with his own lips.'

The first doorman said, 'Go into the palace, you look like a relative of the King.'

Bhumia went in and found his way into the treasury. He collected gold, silver, diamonds, rubies and precious coins and tied them up as a bundle in a sheet. Then he observed a golden box on a shelf. When he picked it up and opened it, he saw that there was something powdered in it. He put his finger in the pot to feel the powder. When he tasted it, rather than being sweet, as he had expected, it turned out to be salty. He remembered again that the Guru had instructed him not to do a bad deed to the people whose salt he took. The stuff in the little box was the King's indigestion remedy.

Bhumia came out of the palace empty-handed but the bundle was left as he had made it.

In the morning the news spread quickly that the king's treasury had been broken into. The king and his ministers hurriedly examined the treasury but to their astonishment nothing had been removed. There was a bundle lying on the floor full of valuables. The king became very concerned and perplexed that a thief had entered his palace and broken into his treasury but left without taking anything away. He checked with the doormen on night duty. One of them mentioned a well dressed man in princely clothes and ornaments whom they allowed to enter, and how he told them that he was a thief and they thought that he was making fun of them. 'He was the only one who went in and then came out after some time and there was nothing suspicious about him,' they echoed.

The king ordered a search but the man was not found. Then

a royal proclamation was made and announcements continued for three days that the king wanted to offer a part of his kingdom to the person who had come to the palace and told the doormen that he was a thief. Still there was no response. Then the king became very frustrated and angry. The next proclamation was that his soldiers should catch and beat up any poor or unemployed people they saw on their rounds. Bhumia heard the news that poor people were going to be beaten and tortured and he remembered the promise he had made to Guru Nanak. He presented himself to the king and begged, 'Please release the poor. Please, please do not torture them or beat them. Do what you want to me. I'm your thief and I'll answer all your questions.'

When the king heard this appeal, he allowed the poor to go and then asked Bhumia, 'Tell me why did you leave my treasury without taking anything from there? What came to your mind that you did what you did?'

Bhumia respectfully answered, 'My king, I am very pleased that I've found the Ultimate Guru.'

The King questioned him further, 'How do you recognise him? What are his distinctive features?'

Bhumia then told the king the story of his encounter with Guru Nanak and the promises he had made to the Guru.

The king felt happy with Bhumia's reply and complimented

him, 'You are great and your Guru is especially great who has taught you so well, and your trust in the Guru is immense. Because of your action, I am very happy with you and make you my Prime Minister.' The king gave him a robe of honour as well.

After a few days, the king requested Bhumia to accept him as his disciple. Bhumia humbly responded, 'Dear King, I am trying to be a disciple myself, so how can you be mine? If you wish, you should build a pilgrim's place in the name of Guru Nanak. Serve the visiting pilgrims well and you will thereby gain much spiritual merit. Guru Nanak knows the hearts and minds of people. If you pray, He will bless you by His presence.

Thus a thief became a saint, whose actions converted others to lead a virtuous life.

The above story (adapted from Bhai Bala Janamsakhi, p. 266–9) in many ways illustrates the value placed within the Sikh faith on three key principles. These are:

❦Meditation and prayer.

❦Earning an honest living through hard work.

❦Sharing with others and service to others.

Five key weaknesses/evils that lead us away from God

- *Kaam (lust)*
- *Krodh (anger)*
- *Lobh (greed)*
- *Moh (attachment/ possessiveness)*
- *Ahunkar (ego)*

LUST AND anger deteriorate the body as borax melts gold.

GURU GRANTH SAHIB, *p. 932*

O GOD, RID us of lust, anger, greed and lies.

GURU GRANTH SAHIB, *p. 932*

WANT TO give up
Want to give up and gain goodness
Give up lust, anger and greed.

GURU GRANTH SAHIB, *p. 1026*

TRUTH IS the foremost, but higher than truth is truthful living.

JAPJI SAHIB, *Guru Granth Sahib, p. 1*

Honest Earning and Other Key Principles ✢ 125

THE POOR AND HUMAN DIGNITY

A POOR PERSON'S mouth is God's treasure chest.

SURAJ PARKASH

THE LORD stands for us if we are not usurpers.

HE WHO strokes his beard in front of the poor, God will burn it in fire.

GURU GRANTH SAHIB, p. 199

The three quotes above show the way to God by serving the poor. A person who shows off his riches and behaves arrogantly in front of a poor person will not be spared by God. Exploitation of others is forbidden.

Nanak says that taking away the rights of another is banned in the same way as pork is banned for Muslims and beef is for Hindus.

WHEN ONE is in extreme hardship
And no one offers help
When relatives flee and enemies surround
When all support and hope takes wing
Remember the Supreme Lord
And no hot [ill] wind shall come.

The Lord is the strength of the weak
Eternal, unborn, undying is the Lord
Revealed as True
Through the Guru's word.

When one is weakened with pangs of poverty and hunger,
Has no money and is not consoled by anyone
When there is no one to help and all work comes to
    nothing
Remember the Supreme Lord
And gain everlasting kingdom.

GURU GRANTH SAHIB, *p. 70*

GOD ALWAYS looks after the weak,
Protects believers and destroys evil.

Birds, beasts, snakes, mountains and kings;
God cares for all forever

Sees all beings in the sea and on land
Does not dwell on their past sinful deeds

Benevolent to the poor, an ocean of compassion
Watches sinners but does not stop bestowing gifts on
   them.

GURU GOBIND SINGH, *Dasam Granth, Swayyai*

O KING! who would come to you?
I have seen such love in the poor Bidar
That I like him
Watching your elephants you are lost in doubt
And don't understand the Sovereign Lord
For me Bidar's offer of water is like nectar
Compared to your milk
His cooked greens are as good as your rice pudding

And I spent the night in singing God's praises
Kabir's master is full of joy and fun
Does not go for status or class.

Guru Granth Sahib, *p. 1105*

Feeding the hungry is a real bargain

ONE DAY young Nanak was sitting at home in a mystic way, busy in his own thoughts when his father Mehta Kalu came home from outside. He saw that his son was still carrying on with his deviant ways. He was very upset and said to Nanak, 'My son, your otherworldliness is troubling me and I feel hurt inside but you don't understand.'

Nanak replied, 'Father, please forgive me. From now on I will do as it pleases you.'

Then Kalu said, 'You should do some business.'

Nanak said, 'Very well, father.'

At this Kalu told Nanak to take twenty rupees (gold coins – a lot of money at that time) and said, 'Buy something really worthwhile, a good bargain. If you do it well once, I'll give you more money.'

Nanak said, 'Fine by me, father. You'll see how I make a good bargain.'

Then Kalu gave the twenty gold coins to Nanak, and called Bhai Bala and said to him, 'Listen Bala, you are sensible and mature. You go with Nanak so that he learns to do business. You are his friend.'

At this Bhai Bala picked up Guru Nanak's things and took the money and they began their journey. Kalu himself went quite a bit of the way with them giving instructions to Nanak: 'Son! I would like you to take over my business during my lifetime, so that my mind feels at ease. When you were born, I felt a great confidence that you would earn much more than what I earn at present. That would make me rich and famous. So you learn the trade of your family and earn many riches, then in my mind I'll feel much happier and contented. So remember that you are going to make a bargain,'

After that Kalu decided to return home. While Nanak and Bala went forward, Kalu occasionally looked back to see them going ahead. Guru Nanak and Bala were having a conversation on the way in which Guru Nanak told Bala stories about the love of God, wisdom and detachment from material goods. After covering over twelve miles they entered a wooded area where they saw a large group of holy men. Some were doing penance, some were sitting on the ground with their arms up in the air,

some standing, some in lotus position, some round a fire keeping themselves warm, some in loin cloths, some had abandoned clothes completely, some were sitting in water, some reading books, some had vowed not to speak. Those who want a good life hereafter have turned their backs on the good life in their present life. Amongst all the holy people was their leader sitting on a deer skin, leaves covering him as a loin cloth and with a jewelled crown on his head, while his mind was on the Divine Sovereign of the world. One sadhu was reading a book by his side.

Seeing this gathering of holy men, Guru Nanak stopped to observe them and then said to Bhai Bala, 'There is no better business than this business. I cannot leave this priceless business. Let's offer this money to these men so that they can have food and clothes, which will make them happy.'

When Bhai Bala heard these words, he replied, 'I'm afraid of your father, Mehta Kalu. He gave you money for trade and his temperament is foul. You know what to do and you will have to deal with your father. I do not wish to get into a row with him. Otherwise I'll do as you tell me.' Then he passed on the money to Guru Nanak.

The Guru went to sit near the holy ascetics, offered his respects and said to them in a humble and kind manner, 'You are not wearing any clothes. Do you not have them or not wear them? You suffer with extreme heat, cold weather and monsoon rain and there is only applied ash on your body.'

Hearing this the ascetic replied, 'We are humble sadhus, we should abstain from clothes. Why are you asking these questions?'

Then Bhai Bala reminded Guru Nanak about buying the provisions, which his father had asked them to do.

Guru Nanak responded, 'Bala, Dad asked me to make a good bargain. You also guide me to buy something good.'

Bala then said, 'You are the son, he is the father; what else can I say?'

At this Guru Nanak addressed the ascetic again: 'Respected holy man, you do not wear clothes, which is fine by me. Does this mean that you don't take food either?'

The ascetic replied, 'Young child! We eat what God sends us. We are hermits and we live in forests. We don't live in towns or villages.'

Nanak then asked him, 'What is your name?'

The hermit answered, 'My name is Reyn [dust of the feet of holy people].' The Guru was pleased with the hermit's reply and then he turned to Bala and remarked, 'I cannot give up this high quality bargain. There is no loss of value in it, only more merit.'

Bala retorted, 'It's between you and Kalu. How should I know whether it is a good or a bad bargain?'

Nanak handed the money to the hermit as an offering.

The hermit then said to Guru Nanak, 'O child! money is of no use to us. Your father has given these coins for trading. Why are you giving them to recluses? You are too young and your work is already decided by your father, you can't give money to us.'

Nanak maintained, 'Listen O holy man, my father sent me to do a good deed, make a good bargain. I think that this is a good bargain; other bargains are unworthy.'

Then the hermit requested that Nanak take back the money, since it would not feed them. Nanak then decided to go to a town nearby and bought groceries such as flour, rice, butter, milk, vegetables, beans, spices and cooking pots and brought them to the place where the ascetics were and put those things in front of them. On seeing all that foodstuff before them, the hermit was very moved and said, 'You are divine. For the last seven days, we have had nothing to eat; we are very hungry. O embodiment of contentment and peace, with your generosity we have plenty.'

Then the young Guru returned home, having achieved a real bargain, that of feeding the poor and the hungry.

From JANAM SAKHI, *Bhai Bala, abridged*

Sajjan Thug, the assassin

GURU NANAK arrived in the country of thugs. There lived a man called Sajjan the Thug (literally a friendly criminal) and he had built his houses around thoroughfares. He had also built a mosque on one side of the house and a temple on the other side. If a Muslim came that way, he would provide a shelter in the mosque and if a Hindu came, that person was helped in the temple. At night they were provided beds in his house. When they were asleep, they were killed with a noose round their necks and then their bodies were thrown in a well and all their belongings taken by him. At daybreak, Sajjan would sit on a prayer carpet with a rosary in his hand. When Guru Nanak, Mardana and I arrived at his place, Sajjan laid on tremendous hospitality. He told his men that these people were full of mystery, since their faces were radiant. When the day passed and the night came, he requested the Guru and us to come indoors and have a comfortable sleep. Guru Nanak asked him his name. He replied, 'Sajjan'.

Guru Nanak then told him, 'You have served us well. You should serve the Supreme One. We'll go to bed after prayers.'

Sajjan said, 'That's alright, but it's getting very late at night.'

Then the Guru composed this hymn while Mardana played on his rebeck on the Guru's instructions:

> Bronze is shiny and bright
> Rub it and jet black emerges
> Washing does not make it pure
> Even if you wash a hundred times
>
> Friends are those
> Who walk when I walk
> Where accounts are taken
> They are seen there standing
>
> Houses, buildings, mansions
> With beautiful wall paintings
> Are but uninhabitable
> And empty ruins
>
> The white feathered herons
> Live in pools of pilgrimage
> They eat living things by tearing them
> So they can't be called really white

My body is like a tall fruitless tree
Seeing me, the beings overlook my shortcomings
The fruits are inedible,
Nor is my body of any use

The blind man has carried a heavy load
And the hilly route is long
I see with my eyes but can't find the way
How can I climb across the hill?

'Of what benefit are workings, virtues
And other clever actions
If you don't hold on to remembering God,' says Nanak
'That action alone will release you from your chains.'

GURU GRANTH SAHIB, *p. 729*

As a result of beholding Guru Nanak and listening to his singing, Sajjan realised that his sins would be revealed; he was transformed and fell on Guru Nanak's feet. He begged the Guru to forgive his sins. The Guru told him that sins are forgiven in God's court by two actions. Sajjan humbly requested the Guru, 'Please show me the means by which my sins can be removed.'

The Guru very kindly said to Sajjan, 'First of all, speak the truth about all the murders you have committed.

He responded, 'Truthfully, I've committed really horrendous murders in my life and I'm very sorry. I don't know how to repent.'

The Guru then told him, 'Collect all the things you stole from the people you killed and bring them here.'

Sajjan honoured the Guru's command and brought all the stolen things and piled them in front of the Guru.

At this the Guru told Sajjan, 'In the Name of God, distribute all these things to the needy.'

Sajjan duly performed the charitable act and began reciting praises of the Guru. Such was the transformation that he became a famous disciple of Guru Nanak. From a conceited thug, he became a man of good conduct and brought many to a virtuous way of living.

From JANAM SAKHI, *Bhai Bala, adapted*

JUSTICE

ONE IN whose heart exists the pride of status or rule
Is like a greedy dog, to be placed in hell.
One who is arrogant about his own youthfulness and
    beauty
Will be born as a worm of excreta.
One who calls himself virtuous
Shall transmigrate in countless forms.
One who is proud of riches or land
Is stupid, blind and ignorant.
One in whose heart, with God's grace, humility resides
Shall be saved here and enjoy eternal peace there.

So long as one stays attached to selfish desires
So long shall the divine judge punish.
The fetters of mammon are broken with the grace of God
The ego is removed with the blessing of the Guru.

SUKHMANI, *verse 1*

GOOD AND bad deeds shall be narrated before the God of
    justice
Some will be brought in closer to God
Others pushed away accounting for their actions.
Those who have prayed, toiled appropriately
Will leave with radiant faces
Many more will be emancipated with them, says Nanak.

JAPJI, Guru Granth Sahib, p. 8

FARID, THE farmer, desires the sweet grapes of Bijour
But sows the seeds of a thorn tree
Spends his life spinning wool
And expects to wear silk.

GURU GRANTH SAHIB, P. 1379

ONE COURT shall judge all
One pen shall record
And we and you meet
In that Divine Court
Accounts are scrutinised
The sinners are crushed
Like seeds in an oil-press.

GURU GRANTH SAHIB, *p. 473*

BY SERVING the One who is peace
Let's pray to that Sovereign.
Why do you do evil deeds
When you know you will reap what you sow?
Do no wrong, be farsighted
Play such a game that you do not lose with God
And serve in such a way that brings merit.

GURU GRANTH SAHIB, *p. 474*

WHAT'S IN the mind comes forth
Spoken words are of little use –
Sowing poison and demanding nectar
What type of justice is this?

GURU GRANTH SAHIB, *p. 474*

CREATOR! YOU are the same Creator of all equally
If the strong attacks another equally strong
Then there is no complaint, no grievance
But when the fierce tiger preys on the helpless cattle
Then the shepherd must explain!

GURU GRANTH SAHIB, *p. 86*

REAL EDUCATION

GOOD EDUCATION is about doing good to others.

GURU GRANTH SAHIB, p. 356

IF HUNDREDS of moons rise
A thousand suns shine
With so much light
Still there is total darkness
Without the Guru.
[The spiritual teacher – remover of the darkness of
    ignorance]

Nanak, they who think not of the Guru
And consider themselves bright
Are like husk left in the field.
Left in the field, claimed by hundreds
They fruit and flower
But within them, in fact, are ashes.

GURU GRANTH SAHIB, p. 463

DIVINE WISDOM is not sought by just talking
To explain, it is hard as steel
Only through grace, is it received
The rest is useless
It is mere telling and method.

GURU GRANTH SAHIB, *p. 465*

O MIND, listen to the Guru's instruction
Then you shall attain God, the Lord of virtues

GURU AMARDAS, *Guru Granth Sahib, p. 512*

THE BOOKS describe God as true
God is neither male nor female
What is the point of reading and debating
When you don't develop understanding in your mind?
God lies hidden in every heart
Behold within your mind
God is in both Hindus and Turks [Muslims]
Kabir proclaims this aloud.

GURU GRANTH SAHIB, *p. 483*

ONE MAY read and read
And fill up a carriage with books,
One may read and read
The whole diverse stock,
One may read and read
And fill boats up with books,
One may read and read
And fill up the pits with books.
Those who read year on year,
Those who read month on month,
Many read life-long
Many read with every breath
Nanak, only one thing is counted
All else is pomposity of 'I-am-ness'.

The more one writes and writes and reads
The more that person displays anger.
The more a person does pilgrimages
The more he talks [without substance].

You read books
Do evening prayers and argue.

GURU GRANTH SAHIB, *p. 467*

HEALING

GOD DOES not let His servant suffer the difficult hour
Such is His prerogative
God puts His healing Hand upon His people
Sustains them in every breath.

I am attached to God
Saviour in the beginning
Saviour at the end and always
Magnificent is my friend.

Seeing the wonder of God
I feel happy as a blossom
Pray, pray and be happy
Says Nanak, the Lord has fully saved me.

GURU GRANTH SAHIB, *p. 682*

THE KIND master has broken my bonds
God is a merciful protector of the meek.

The Perfect Guru has shown benevolence
And removed my malady.

My mind and body are at peace and joyful
God is worthy of worship.
God's name is the medicine
Having which, no sickness attacks.

In the company of holy people,
Mind and body become full of love of God
And there is no pain and suffering thereafter.

Concentrating internally,
I meditate on the God of many Names
Sins are removed and become pure
In the shelter of the holy.

All misfortune is removed
All misfortune goes away
Listening to and reciting God's praises
Nanak utters the sublime Name
And sings God's praises.

GURU ARJAN, *Guru Granth Sahib, p. 814*

THE CREATOR Guru has removed my fever
I am deeply grateful to the True Guru
Who has preserved my honour in the whole world

Placing his hand on its forehead
The Guru has saved the child

God has given the nectar of Eternal Name
Compassionate God protected his servant's dignity
Nanak says, 'What the Guru utters
Is accepted in God's court.'

GURU ARJAN, *Guru Granth Sahib, p. 821*

THE GURU blessed the eyes with light
Doubts disappeared and the service fully accepted
God saved it from smallpox
God's grace caused it.
Nanak says, 'One who prays, lives
In the company of the holy and
Takes the water of immortality.'

GAURI 5, *Guru Granth Sahib*

CREATOR HAS brought peace and coolness
Fever has left the family
The perfect spiritual master has saved.

The protection of the True One was sought
The Supreme God became the Protector
Peace, poise and happiness developed in no time

Mind is at peace
God's name, God's name given as cure
It took away all ills.

GURU GRANTH SAHIB, *p. 622–3*

PEACE HAS come
The Lord has caused it
High fever and sins have gone,
My brother.

Repeat the Lord's name
Daily with your tongue
Reflect on the qualities
Of the unfathomable Lord.

Healing ☙ 153

In the company of the righteous
Salvation is obtained
Sing regularly every day
The praises of the Pure.

Your suffering ceases and be saved, my friend
Concentrate your mind
Remember your own God with word and deed
Nanak seeks your shelter, O Lord!

GURU GRANTH SAHIB, *p. 200*

ILLNESS IS gone
God took it away
I can sleep now
Peace, happiness
And equipoise have entered my home.

O my brothers, eat as much as you can
Reflect in your mind the Immortal Name
Nanak takes the refuge of the perfect Guru
Who has maintained the esteem of His Name.

GURU ARJAN, *Guru Granth Sahib, p. 807*

HOT [ILL] wind blows not
Under God's protection
God's protective circle is around me
On all four sides
And I do not feel pain, O brother
I have met the perfect Guru
Who caused the creation
Has given me the medicine
Of God's name and
I concentrated on the One God

The Saviour has saved me
And cured me of my ills
Nanak says, God through His grace
Has protected me.

GURU GRANTH SAHIB, *p. 819*

TAKE A bath, pray to our Lord
Both mind and body are healed.

Countless obstacles are removed
In the protection of God
And good things emerge.

The Lord's words and speech are bewitching
O brothers, sing them, hear them, read them
The Perfect Guru will save you.

The True Master's greatness cannot be measured
The Compassionate Lord is the love of His devotees.
God has been maintaining the dignity of His saints
Since the beginning of Time, their care is His essential
    character.

Savour the ambrosial food of God's Name
Put it into your mouth at all times.

The frailty of old age, death and fever
Shall run away, when you sing about the qualities of God
    every day.

My Lord heard my prayer
All my issues are resolved.

Manifest is the glory of Guru Nanak,
In the Whole Wide World.

GURU GRANTH SAHIB, *p. 611*

501/-PARKASH KOUR W/o S. SWARN SINGH
BHATIA KRISHNA S.G. 54 A. ASR

۵۵.۰ روپے کی سیوا عاشیر اولا بنتر محمد عبداللہ پیرانی ویلی

لرائی فٹو بیندر رنگ اثر شرن نے کرائی

THOSE PEOPLE who seem great
Suffer from the illness of stress.
Can any one be great by being rich?
Great is the one who is in tune with God.

Landowners usually fight over land
Their desire is unquenched, though they know that
    death is near.
Nanak says, 'I reflected and arrived at this conclusion
That there is no relief without prayer and meditation.'

GURU GRANTH SAHIB, *p. 188*

COMPASSION

ALL HAVE precious minds
Do not ever break them.

If you desire your beloved God
Do not break any heart.

GURU GRANTH SAHIB, *p. 1384*; FARID, *130*

NEAR THE day of the new moon
Behold God
Control the five senses
Listen to prayers
Have contentment in your mind
And compassion towards all beings.
In this way your fasting will be complete
Concentrate your wandering mind on the One God
With pure mind and body, meditate
The Supreme God resides in all
Nanak sings God's praises
Let this be your eternal faith.

GURU GRANTH SAHIB, *p. 299*

MAKE COMPASSION your cotton wool
Contentment, your thread
Chastity, your knot
Strength of will, the twist
If you have such a thread of life
Only then put it on me, O Pandit!

GURU NANAK, *Asa Di Var*

LET COMPASSION be your mosque
Let faith be your prayer mat
Let honest living be your Qur'an
Let modesty be the rules of observance
Let piety the fast you keep
Thus strive to be a Muslim.
Right conduct be the Kaaba
Truth the Prophet
Good deeds your prayer
Submission to God's will your rosary.
Nanak if you do this
The Lord will be your protector.

GURU GRANTH SAHIB, *p. 140*

160 ❦ *Human Life*

Bhai Kanhayya

Bhai Kanhayya was a disciple of the tenth Guru, Gobind Singh. He was born in 1648 in Sodhara in Sialkot District, which is now in Pakistan, the son of a wealthy trader. Instead of following the family trade, he preferred the company of religious people in search of spiritual fulfilment. Once on his travels, he had the opportunity to see Guru Tegh Bahadur, became inspired and chose to be the Guru's Sikh (follower). He then settled down by building a centre for pilgrims and visitors who were served there without any distinction of religion or caste. In 1705 he again visited Anandpur, to pay respects to the then Guru, Gobind Singh, son of Guru Tegh Bahadur. He saw that the mighty Mughal imperial army and the forces of the hill kingdoms had joined together and attacked the Guru and his small group of guards. Bhai Kanhayya saw many wounded and dying in the field crying for water to relieve their thirst. Bhai Kanhayya started serving water to everybody who needed it without distinction of friend or enemy. This made the fighting Sikhs very angry because they felt that Bhai Kanhayya was helping the enemy to maintain their strength. Some of them reported Bhai

Kanhayya to the Guru. The Guru asked him to explain his action. Bhai Kanhayya replied, 'I don't see any friend or foe. I only see you demanding water, my Lord.' The Guru was so pleased with Bhai Kanhayya that he also gave him ointment to tend the wounds. The Guru, thereby, demonstrated to the other Sikhs that Bhai Kanhayya rightly understood his teachings. In this way the Sikh Red Cross was created early in the eighteenth century. There is an order among the Sikhs following in the footsteps of Bhai Kanhayya, known as Sevapanthis, *literally meaning the 'Selfless Servers'*.

RECONCILIATION

IN THE company of saints and holy people
No more is there a feeling of 'us' and 'them'.

No one an enemy, none a stranger
I get along with all.

What God wills is good
I received this sublime wisdom
By being with holy people.

One God pervades all
Nanak beholds and blossoms with joy.

GURU ARJAN, *Guru Granth Sahib, p. 1299*

AS A child intentionally or unintentionally
Commits countless bad deeds

The father tells it off, scolds,
Teaches and explains in many ways
Then holds and hugs the child.

In similar ways, God blesses,
Forgives past sins
And shows the right way.

GURU ARJAN, *Guru Granth Sahib, p. 624–5*

COUNTLESS WRONGS, does the son
His mum forgives, and remembers none.

KABIR, *Guru Granth Sahib, p. 478*

FAITHFUL FOLLOWER
(GURSIKH)

DEFINING A SPIRITUAL SIKH

ONE WHO wants to be called a Sikh of the True Guru
Should awake early each morning and meditate upon
　　God,
Be alert, before dawn,
Bathe in the sacred pool [of Amritsar] of immortality,
Concentrate on the Guru's teachings and recite prayers
　　to God,
Sing the Guru's hymns at the daybreak
And remember God while sitting and standing [doing
　　daily routines].
That Sikh who repeats the Name with every breath
Becomes dear to the Guru.
On whom my Master showers grace
That follower hears the sermon from the Guru,
Nanak, the humble servant, yearns for the dust of the feet
　　of that disciple
Who prays and helps others to pray.

GURU GRANTH SAHIB, *p. 305*

GURMUKH – GURUWARDS

THERE IS peace within a follower humbly facing towards
   the Guru –
Imbued with the Name in body and mind,
Thinks of the Name, reads of the Name
Concentrates on the Name
Receives the wealth of the Name
And stress goes away
Meets the true Guru, the Name grows
Desire and hunger all go away
The Name is obtained.

GURU GRANTH SAHIB, *p. 1317*

In the above hymn the phrase 'The Name' stands for God.

GOD STANDS alongside for the work of His holy people
God Himself comes to work with them.

GURU GRANTH SAHIB, *p. 783*

THE GURMUKH way is the true way
Which gently roots in a disciple's home.
The *gurmukh* way is the true wealth
Which gathers as dust on feet.
The Guru's follower's bathing
Is to receive Guru's wisdom
And to remove the filth of bad thoughts.
The worship of the true disciple
Is to respect and to love another.
The obedience of the Guru's disciple
Is to treasure the Guru's preaching.
As a precious garland round the neck
The living of a Guru's disciple
Is to live like the dead without pride
And to reflect on the Guru's word.

BHAI GURDAS, *Var 28, Pauri 9*

LET THERE be storm
Let there be gale
Let it be raining cats and dogs –
Must go and see the Guru.
Let the sea, the ocean be deep and salty
A Guru's follower will cross it to get to the Guru

Gurmukh – *Guruwards* 169

As a human dies without water
So does the disciple die without the Guru.
As the earth blossoms with rain
So does the disciple on meeting the Guru.
A servant should be ever-ready to serve.
Again and again call and pray.
Nanak prays to God:
For meet the Guru and be at peace.

GURU GRANTH SAHIB, *pp. 757–8*

ONE WHEN in grief
Does not accept grief
Is not engrossed in comfort,
Attachment and fear
Realises gold as only dust.

Untouched by blame or praise
Or by greed, desire and egomania,
Stays above joy or sorrow
Unaffected by acclaim or accusation.

Discards all desire or longing,
Stays aloof from the world,

170 ⚬ *Faithful Follower (Gursikh)*

Remains untouched by lust or anger
In whose heart the creator abides.

Only that person understands this way of life
On whom the Guru showers grace
Nanak says, 'That person's soul merges with the divine
As water merges with water.'

GURU TEGH BAHADUR, *Guru Granth Sahib, pp. 633–4*

THE TRUE devotee (*gurmukh*) self-improves
And leaves for the Divine court.
Going in the true court of the Divine,
Occupies a true place of honour.
The true devotee's true food is
To cherish Divine wonder in trust.
The true devotee has a stable mind,
Is unmoved under strain.
The true devotee speaks the truth
And good things ever.
The true devotees go when called
And come when sent [by God].

BHAI GURDAS, *Var 19, Pauri 14*

Gurmukh – *Guruwards* ✦ 171

THE FOUR things [moral values, wealth, desire and liberation]
Stand and wait for the order of the *gurmukh*.
The four directions, all bound by the divine thread,
Prostrate before him/her.
Vedas do not understand the mystery
The pandits read and read and the listeners listen and listen to no avail.
In the four ages of time, the divine light glows
From the four castes, there is one of the *gursikh*.
They celebrate the days of the Gurus and sow the beneficial seeds of spiritual merit
In the congregation all are equal [grandparents and grandchildren, too].

BHAI GURDAS, *Var 29, verses 5–6*

PEACE FOR A SIKH

PRAY, PRAY, pray
And be at peace.

GURU GRANTH SAHIB, *p. 262*

AWAKE IN peace
Stay in peace
There is no fear
With such understanding.
One God is our master, our saviour
Who knows the hearts and minds of all.
Sleep carefree, awake carefree
Because here and beyond, you abide O Lord!
Peace prevails at home
Peace abounds outside
Nanak says, 'Because the Guru taught the practice.'

GURU GRANTH SAHIB, *p. 1136*

THERE IS no peace with earning more wealth
There is no peace in watching dance and drama
There is no peace in working in many countries
There is complete peace in singing the praises of God,
    our Lord !
Get peace, equipoise and bliss
With good fortune, find the holy congregation
Where all Guru-facing people recite the Name of God.

GURU GRANTH SAHIB, *p. 225*

ENJOY IMMENSE peace
By meditating on God.
Numerous diseases disappear
By singing the glories of God.
Inner peace develops
By concentrating on the Lord.
All wishes are fufilled
By keeping the Name in mind.

Obstacles are removed
By self effacing,
Receiving the gift of wisdom
And understanding from the Guru.
Those to whom God gives
Receive in abundance
You are the Sovereign of all
All are in Your protection.

GURU GRANTH SAHIB, p. 520

AS THE pillars strengthen a temple
So does the Guru's Word stabilise the mind.

GURU GRANTH SAHIB, p. 263

176 ☙ *Faithful Follower (Gursikh)*

THE VALUE OF SANGAT
(CONGREGATIONAL WORSHIP)

TREES THAT grow near the sandalwood tree become
   perfumed as sandal
Metals touched by philosopher's stone become gold
Rivers and streams going into the Ganges become the
   Ganges
So does the Sangat save sinners and wash away their
   sins,
Saving countless souls from the hell fires
And the holy see God in there.

GURU GRANTH SAHIB, *p. 1365*

MY BROTHERS, let's meet together
Remove double-mindedness
And concentrate on the love of God.

Let there be attachment to God's Name
O holy folks, spread your mats and be seated.

In this way play the game of chess, O brother!
As a person of faith, recite the name of God day and night
To save you from suffering pain at the time of death.

Your actions and your faith be your chess-board
And the truth your dice
Win over lust, anger, greed and attachment
Such a game is dear to God.

Awake early before dawn and take a bath
Before going to bed, remember God.
My True Lord will save you from dangerous moves
You will reach home with peace and contentment.

God Himself plays, Himself watches,
Has on His own, made all Creation.
O Nanak, that being of God who plays by His rules
Wins the game of living and returns home eternal.

GURU ARJAN, *Guru Granth Sahib, p. 1185*

WHO SHOULD be considered the true community of faith?
Where there is discourse about the one God
There is the Order to worship the only Name
Nanak, the true Guru has solved this mystery.

GURU GRANTH SAHIB, *p. 72*

The Value of Sangat (Congregational Worship) ❧ 179

THE HAPPY king, Hari Chand, had an attractive queen, named Tara, with pretty eyes

She used to go to listen to the holy congregation singing God's praises.

Once while she was out the king woke up, it was after midnight;

Not seeing his queen, he was completely perplexed.

Another night [the king stayed awake but pretended to be asleep and] followed his young wife.

The queen arrived at the congregation place

And the king took away one of her clogs as evidence.

She worshipped God as she normally did

And, after the service, there was her pair of clogs for her to wear as usual

The king wondered at this added clog and realised that, a special miracle of faith had occurred.

Let's be a sacrifice to the company of the holy.

GURU GRANTH SAHIB, *Var 10, Pauri 6, p. 375*

CONGREGATION OF the holy
Is the sphere of truth
Where the understanding of the Formless
And the Word is gained
To stay grateful for the Creator
In nature.

BHAI GURDAS, Ballad 16, section 12

KABIR, DIALOGUE with devotees is beneficial
For an hour or half, or even half of half an hour.

GURU GRANTH SAHIB, p. 1377

TWENTY POINTS to the Guru
Twenty-one points to the congregation.

Sikh saying, oral tradition since Guru Arjan's time

This means that the congregation achieves more points because the Guru resides in the congregation, the community of faith, rather than on His own.

ALL ARE free to enter the Gurdwara without any consideration of caste or creed. No intoxicant or any obnoxious thing such as tobacco or alcohol is allowed to be taken in.

Smoking is prohibited amongst the Sikhs as part of Sikh observance and is usually referred to as the 'World Polluter'.

Sikh Code of Conduct

THE KHALSA

Wheguru ji ka Khalsa, Waheguru ji ki Fateh is a Sikh greeting shared by Sikhs and is always repeated at the start and end of an address or hymn singing in the Gurdwara, the Sikh place of worship. It literally means that the Khalsa (the community of initiated Sikhs) are God's and victory will be to God.

The Creation of the Khalsa, on Baisakhi day in 1699 by Guru Gobind Singh, is usually celebrated on 13 April by the Sikh community everywhere in the world. Khalsa stands for the ultimate joining together of the spiritual and temporal in all its purity and the best of human values. Khalsa represents a visual symbol of equality without distinctions of high or low birth, male or female, area, language or culture and encapsulates saintliness, engagement in everyday human struggles, preparedness and vigilance to fight injustice and to protect the poor and needy. The first five people that were chosen symbolised values required to establish a universal community of the virtuous – people with compassion, righteousness, courage, majesty and detachment and who were full of the love of God. Guru Gobind Singh describes the Khalsa as follows:

KHALSA IS my special form
Khalsa is among whom I live
Khalsa is my key part
Khalsa is always where I am
Khalsa is my love sublime
Khalsa is my saving kind
Khalsa is my commitment and honour
Khalsa is my superior peace
Khalsa is my close friend
Khalsa is mother and father giving comfort
Khalsa is my respect and dignity
Khalsa is my always affectionate mate
Khalsa is my family, my prestige
Khalsa is from whom I rose
Khalsa is my mansion, my treasure
Khalsa has led to my respect
Khalsa is my own people, my own family
Khalsa gives me liberation
Khalsa is my body, my life
Khalsa is my life's soul
Khalsa has my pride and importance
Khalsa has my interest
Khalsa provides for me
Khalsa is my body, my breath

Khalsa is my righteousness and action
Khalsa is my secret, my confidante
Khalsa is my complete True Guru
Khalsa is my companion, the brave
Khalsa is my knowledge, my wisdom
Khalsa is on whom I concentrate
Khalsa's praises cannot be said
One tongue cannot express it fully
The many tongues of the serpent Sheshnag
And the wisdom of the goddess Saraswati
Are still not capable of describing its qualities
I haven't seen an iota of untruth in it
The Supreme God and Guru Nanak are my witnesses
Khalsa's glories, I may be able to sing
If every pore of my skin turns into a tongue
I am Khalsa's, Khalsa is mine
Merged in each other as a drop in the ocean
Khalsa is the army of The Immortal
Khalsa emerged out of the Supreme Soul's will
As long as Khalsa stays unique
I give it total radiance

If it follows a different divisive way
I won't put my trust in it.

From Sarab Loh Granth

Serving them is of value,
Serving others is not so good
Giving in charity to them is good
No other charity giving is better
Giving to them in charity leads to growth in merit
All other giving is of little value
What is in my home is due to them
Body, mind and wealth.

With their blessing, many victories are won
With their blessing, alms are given
With their blessing, all sins are removed
With their blessing, homes are full
With their blessing, good education is gained
With their blessing, foes are no more
With their blessing, I'm adorned
Otherwise there are millions of poor like me.

Guru Gobind Singh, *Gian Prabodh, verse 645*

GOOD LIFE

The following is a hymn in which Guru Nanak converses with his father and with God about everyday matters and his view of happiness.

ALL TASTES are sweet, if one believes
Savoury to listen
Sour-sweet to speak
Spicy to sing
Thirty-six special ambrosial tastes are for that being
On whom God casts the gracious glance.

O father! that eating destroys happiness
Which causes pain to the body and leads to evil passions.
To be immersed in the love of God is the same as wearing
    red*
To give in charity is like wearing white
To remove the darkness of evil is my wearing of sky blue.
And to meditate on God ['s feet] is my robe of honour
Your Name is my wealth and my youth, O Lord
And contentment, my waistband.

---

* Red is the colour of celebration in Indian tradition; a bride usually wears red on her wedding day.

O father! such wearing of clothes destroys happiness
Which causes agony to the body and leads to evil
passions.
To know Your way is my horse, the saddle and gold livery
To go after virtues is for me as are arrows, quiver, bow,
spear and sword
My dignity and fame are like music played by army bands
carrying their lances
Your grace, my high caste.

O father! such riding is of no avail for happiness
Mounting which causes injury to the body and leads to
evil passions.
Houses and mansions are blissful happiness of the Name
Your gracious glance, my family
What pleases you is Your Order for me
To say more is beyond my limits
Nanak, the True King does not need advisers
To take decisions.
O father! that sleep is disastrous to happiness
Doing which the body is mangled and the mind is led to
evil passions.

GURU GRANTH SAHIB, *pp. 16–17*

IN WHATEVER home the glory of God is recited
And reflections shared on the Creator
Praises sung, the giver of life worshipped
You sing the glory of my Fearless One!

I make my sacrifice to the Glory
Which leads to eternal peace
Day after day the Divine Protector cares for
And the same Giver gives to all beings

Your gifts are priceless, O God!
Your benefaction beyond measure
The time and day of union is ordained [meeting God after
    death].

Join and pour the oil of good omen on the threshold
Friends, bless the human bride
So that she meets the Master Groom.

KEERTAN SOHILLA, *Guru Granth Sahib, p. 12*

IN LAUGHING, playing, eating and getting ready
While doing all these you have salvation

GURU GRANTH SAHIB, *p. 552*

THREE THINGS are in the platter
Truth, contentment and contemplation.

Added to them is the ambrosial Name
The sustainer of all.

Those who eat and those who savour
Are liberated.

This thing should not be discarded
Keep it ever in your heart.

Holding on to the Lord ['s feet]
Enables us to cross the dark world ocean
Says Nanak, 'All around is the Creator's work.'

GURU GRANTH SAHIB, *p. 1429*

WITHOUT SERVING the True Guru, we suffered unbearable
    pain
And moved constantly in four time zones.
We, your beggars, You the giver in every age
Reveal to us the Word.
Show us Your Mercy
Have us in Your Grace, Our Dear God
Lead us to meet the kind True Teacher
Give us the sustenance of Your Divine Name
There is endless suffering and continuous transmigration
Without serving the True Lord.
We, the poor and lowly,
You the Eternal Benefactor, who sustains all
Control desire, relieve confusion with equipoise
Then only receive the Name, the Sustainer.
With the taste of God's love,
The mind is purified and all troubles end
The selfless in faith attain eternal life.
Then there is no death
The nectar of the Divine Name is forever sweet
And is found in the Word by a few.
Thus God reveals His Eternal secret to those in His grace

Those who are imbued with God's love
Find peace and eternal bliss.

GURU AMARDAS, Guru Granth Sahib, pp. 603–4

THERE IS a place called City-of-no-sorrows
There is no grieving, and no one suffers there.
No tax collectors, no one demands tribute.
There is no worrying or sin or fear or death.
My friends, I have found myself a great place
Where everything is good and everyone is happy.
Where the Sovereignty of the Lord is forever
There all are equal, none second or third.
.It is a populous and famous city
The citizens are prosperous
They move as freely as they please
No state official stops them
Says Ravidas, the emancipated cobbler,
'My fellow citizen is my friend.'

GURU GRANTH SAHIB, p. 345

BLISS

The verses below form part of all Sikh worship.

BLISS HAS dawned, O my mother
I have found the True Guru
The True Guru I have found with ease
Congratulations ring in my mind.

Heavenly musician families with their precious music
Have come to sing the divine Word with me.

Those in whose heart God resides
Sing the song of the holy Word
Says Nanak, 'Bliss is mine
For I have found the True Guru.'

O my mind, ever abide with God
Abide with God, O my mind
All your sorrows will be removed
God will accept you
And all your work will be rendered fruitful.

The sovereign is All-Powerful in all things
Why should you ever forget?
Says Nanak, 'O my mind stay ever with God.'

O True Sovereign, what do you lack in Your home?
There is abundance in Your Home
Those to whom you give, receive
And sing your glory always
Your Name residing in their minds.

In whose minds the Name resides
Resounds heavenly music of the Word
Says Nanak, 'True Sovereign!
What is not in your home?'

The True Name is my sustenance
The True Name sustains me, satisfies my hunger
Abiding in my mind, the True Name
Has granted me peace and joy
And fulfilled all my desires.

I offer my sacrifice to the Guru
Who has granted all these gifts and blessings
Says Nanak, 'Listen O saints, love the Word.
The True Name sustains me.'
In Your blessed house
Five types of heavenly music play the Word
Fortunate is the place in which the Word resounds
And your power resides.

You have curbed the five evils
And removed the fear of death for
Those whom you grace,
Their good actions from the beginning
Have followed Your Name.
Says Nanak, 'They gain peace and happiness
And in their homes [hearts] is heard unsung music.'

Listen to this song of bliss and become fortunate
All your wishes shall be granted
Discover the Supreme Transcendent Being
All grief and sorrows leave.

Suffering, sickness and affliction are removed
With listening to the True Word
Friends and saints are all fulfilled
Learning from the Perfect Guru.
Those who hear are made pure
Those who speak are made pure
For they are imbued with the True Guru
Says prayerful Nanak, 'Those who place themselves
At the Guru's feet hear the sounds of Celestial Music.'

GURU AMARDAS, *Anand Sahib, first five verses and final verse*

I DO NOT appreciate what you have done for me, O God!
And made me worthy of your service.
I am worthless and have no qualities
You have taken pity on me
Graced me with a shower of kindness
And I have met my real friend, the true Guru
Nanak, if I receive the blessing of the Name, I live
And my body and soul blossom.

GURU GRANTH SAHIB, *p. 1429*

ACCEPTANCE OF OTHER FAITHS

SOME SAY Rama, Rama
Some say Khudai
Some worship Gosain
Some worship Allah
Some call on the Creator
Some call on the Maker
Some call on the Compassionate
Some call on the Benevolent
Some bathe in the Sacred Rivers
Some go to do Hajj
Some worship, some bow
Some read the Vedas
Some read the Qur'an
Some wear blue
Some wear white
Some call themselves Turks [Muslims]
Some call themselves Hindu
Some are after heaven
Some are after the place of the gods
Nanak says the one who accepted God's command
Is the one who understands the mystery of the Divine.

GURU GRANTH SAHIB, *p. 885*

SOMEONE SHAVES his head and calls himself an ascetic
Another a practitioner of yoga
Another a hermit
Another a celibate
Another a monk.

Some are Hindus
Some are Turks [Muslims]
Some are Shi'a Muslim preachers
Some are Sunni Imams
Ensure that you acknowledge the human race as one.

The Creator called Karta [Hindu name]
And Karim [Muslim name] is the same
The Compassionate and Sustainer is the same
There is no other
Let us not be mistaken or have doubts about another.

Worship only the One God
Who is the Supreme Spiritual teacher of all
All are manifestations of the One Form
All humanity the Embodiment of One Light.

The temple and the mosque are the same
Puja in the temple and *namaz* in the mosque
Is the worship of the same God
All humans are essentially the same
Though they appear to be different.

There are numerous names in numerous places
Of God, deities, angels, demons, devils
As a result of the influence of numerous countries,
Numerous languages and styles of living.

Same eyes
Same ears
Same body
Same facility of speaking
All are made from the same
Earth, air, fire and water.

Allah is the same
Abhekh [Hindu name] is the same
The Qur'an and Puranas are the same
They are about the same
The One God has made them.

AKAL USTAT, *verses 85–86, p. 55–56*

THE TRUTH is the remedy for all, washes away all sins
Nanak prays that faith be his wrap.

GURU NANAK, *Asa Di Var, verse 10,*
Guru Granth Sahib, p. 468

ONE PARENT:
We are all children of that one parent, the God

GURU GRANTH SAHIB, *p. 611*

THE BEST RELIGION

OF ALL religions
The best religion is
To utter the Name of God with adoration
And to do good deeds.

Of all rites
The best rite
Is to cleanse one's mind
In the company of the holy people.

Of all good deeds
The best deed
Is to meditate on the Name
And praise it forever.

Of all speeches
The best speech
Is to listen to and
Then reflect on God with others.

Of all shrines
The most sacred shrine,
Nanak says,
'Is the heart in which God dwells.'

SUKHMANI SAHIB, *verse 3, section 8*; GURU GRANTH SAHIB, *p. 266*

HOW OTHERS VIEW
SIKHISM

THE ADI Granth is part of mankind's common spiritual treasure. It is important that it should be brought within the direct reach of as many people as possible. Few readers of English will have had the opportunity of hearing the Adi Granth being chanted in the Golden Temple of the Sikh religion at Amritsar; and few again of those who have heard the chanting have been in a position to understand its meaning. The Adi Granth is remarkable for several reasons. Of all the religious scriptures, this book is the most highly venerated. It means more to Sikhs than even the Qur'an means to Muslims, the Bible to Christians and the Torah to Jews. The Adi Granth is the Sikhs' perpetual Guru (spiritual guide).

ARNOLD TOYNBEE in *The Sacred Writings of the Sikhs, p. 9*

THE SIKHS are people of their holy book to a greater degree, perhaps than followers of other faiths, for the scripture is also central to the wedding ceremony, is used in the naming of a child, and consulted when decisions have to be made.

W. OWEN COLE *with* PEGGY MORGAN, *Six Religions in the Twentieth Century, p. 111–12*

THE SIKH Gurus who compiled the Adi Granth had this noble quality of appreciation of what was valuable in other religious traditions. The saints belong to the whole world. They are universal men, who free our minds from bigotry and superstition, dogma and ritual and emphasize the central simplicities of religion. The great seers of the world are the guardians of inner values who correct the fanaticism of their superstitious followers.

At a time when men were conscious of failure, Nanak appeared to renovate the spirit of religion and humanity ... Nanak tried to build a nation of self-respecting men and women, devoted to God and their leaders, filled with a sense of equality and brotherhood for all. The gurus are the light-bearers of mankind. They are the messengers of the timeless.

S. RADHAKRISHNAN in *The Sacred Writings of the Sikhs*, pp. 18–19

NANAK PREACHED a religion of the divine Name, and that religion, present in the hymns of superb beauty, has descended through the Sikh community to the present day.

HEW McLEOD, *Sikhism*, p. xxvi

SIKHS BELIEVE that God should always be remembered in the course of everyday life. Guru Nanak taught that truth is above everything, but that truthful living is higher than truth. There are certain ethical principles which are intrinsic to Sikh belief and practice. Foremost amongst these are: *nam japna* (reciting the name), *kirat karna* (earning a living by honest and approved means) and *vand chhakna* (sharing with the needy). *Sewa* (service) to the community at large, or helping to meet the particular need for the benefit of others, is also an essential part of Sikh life.

The concept of equality was of central importance to Guru Nanak Dev. He taught that all people are born with the opportunity to attain *mukti*, regardless of caste or creed and of whether they are rich or poor, male or female, high or low, educated or uneducated. What influences *mukti* is the *karam*, *maya* and *haumai* of individuals and the grace of the Guru in overcoming *haumai* and *maya*. The ten Sikh Gurus did not believe in caste distinctions and taught that every person is equal before God. The Sikh concept of equality embraces women as well as men in both secular and religious life.

RELIGIONS IN THE UK: A MULTI-FAITH DIRECTORY, *ed. Paul Weller,*
p. 610

MOKSHA, THE Sikh ideal of spiritual liberation, extends to an egalitarian and free mode of existence. The free world beyond entails a life without the political, sexual, racial or caste oppressions on earth. Along with the spiritual goal of moksha, the Sikh Gurus tried to formulate new possibilities for the weak and degraded within their society. Their poetic articulations seek a radical transformation of the life of the oppressed, especially women and those of the low caste. Not only were the Sikh Gurus sensitive to their social milieu, they were also engaged in raising the conscience and consciousness of their discordant community. They promoted orthopraxis over orthodoxy, and their theology and spirituality are intertwined with politics.

The Gurus tried particularly to give women status and dignity. They used both paternal and maternal symbolism in their expression of the utterly transcendent Reality, and images of conception, gestation, birth and lactation express the creative force of the Ultimate in Sikh scripture. Guru Nanak and his successors were deeply conscious of the victimisation of women that was prevalent in their society: customs such as *sati* (the immolation of a Hindu widow on the funeral pyre of her husband) or *purdah* (the veiling of women) and a belief in menstrual pollution, were loudly denounced. There is no priesthood in Sikhism, and the sacred text stresses the equality of men and women in their search for the divine. Celibacy is rejected; a wife or a husband is regarded as an essential partner for moral and spiritual development. Rules of conduct and religious duties are the same for both men and women. Both have identical status and as early as the time of Guru Amar Das (1552–74) women were appointed as religious leaders as well as men.

SUSAN STRONGE, *The Arts of the Sikh Kingdoms, p. 142*

THE COMBINATION of piety and practical activity which Guru Nanak manifested in his own life he bequeathed to his followers and it remains characteristic of many who own him as Guru today. At its best it is a piety devoid of superstition and a practical activity compounded with determination and an immense generosity. It explains much that has happened in the Panjab during the last four centuries and it explains much that can be witnessed there today.

W.H. MCLEOD, *Guru Nanak and the Sikh Religion, pp. 231–2*

THE MAIN essence of Guru Nanak's hymns and sermons was to promote the equality of all people before God, which in medieval times meant the equality of all people in their self-improvement. In Kartarpur, Guru Nanak established an order according to which all the members of the community, regardless of caste or creed, had meals together in a circle, inviting all the willing and needy. Amar Das, the third Guru, transformed this collective meal, called the Guru Ka Langar or the Guru's table, into one of the most important Sikh rituals, which is preserved to this day. The Guru's table was a challenge to Hinduism's caste system, for caste rules of ritual purity and ritual pollution are particularly strict in matters of who may accept food with whom. At the same time this ritual serves to consolidate the feeling of solidarity among the Sikhs.

BORIS KLYUEV, *Religion in Indian Society, p. 96*

THE ADVOCATE of Sikhism should not attack the fundamentals of other faiths, and a scrutiny of the Adi Granth shows that it is ritualism and claims to exclusiveness, which are seen to obscure the principles of Islam and Hinduism even in its yogic form, which come in for criticism rather than their basic concepts. The sacred thread and the Vaishnavite hair lock are specifically rejected.

Renunciation is commended but defined as being like lotus in water; worldly activities should be pursued but with detachment. Thus a Sikh should work hard and earn an honest living but also be generous and give in charity. Celibacy is similarly commended and defined. He is celibate who is married to one wife only and treats all other women as sisters and daughters.

W. OWEN COLE, *The Sikhs, p. 124*

THE WILLINGNESS of many Sikhs to work hard is certainly a genuine characteristic, as likewise is the readiness with which they give. One never sees a Sikh beggar and the hospitality of the Sikh people is legendary. Hard work, it is generally believed, brings its own reward, and the kind of immense labour that most Sikhs extend to agriculture is extended to other tasks. The effort put into a religious duty is most impressively seen on the occasional *kar-seva* of the pool surrounding Harimandir Sahib. After the pool has been drained, countless Sikhs come voluntarily for the massive task of cleaning out the silt which has gradually accumulated in the pool as a result of the regular replenishment of water by an underground canal.

HEW MCLEOD, *Sikhism, p. 216*

A PERSONAL EXPERIENCE will illustrate how the ideal of service is developed and practised. Once a group of us were walking around the sacred tank of the Golden Temple in Amritsar, as any foreigner is welcome to do if he keeps his head covered and his feet bare. A couple of Sikhs were accosting all comers with the plea, *Sewa karo, sewa karo,* 'Do a service, do a service.' They were pointing out a row of baskets filled with rubble from building operations. This rubble was to be carried up a ramp and thrown over a wall. This is usually the work of coolies, but it afforded a means of practicing the service ideal, and incidentally, of sharing in the virtue sure to accrue to one helping in the holy work. Well dressed Sikhs, men and women, were carrying baskets up the ramp as we joined them, and a missionary lady principal, a home economics teacher, my fifteen year old daughter, and myself carried our baskets up the ramp. Teja Singh remarks that Gurdwaras are schools for teaching the practice of service to be applied later in the world abroad. People of high families may be seen in the Gurdwaras sweeping the pavements, cleaning utensils, fetching water, or plying large fans.

C.H. LOEHLIN, *The Sikhs and Their Scriptures, p. 20*

NANAK LOFTILY invokes the Lord as the one, the sole, timeless being; the creator, the self-existent, the incomprehensible, and the everlasting. He likens the Deity to Truth, which was before the world began, which is and which shall endure for ever as the ultimate idea or cause of all we know or behold. He addresses equally the Mulla and the Pandit, the Dervish and the Sannyasi that Lord of Lords who has seen come and go numberless prophets, Vishnus and Sivas. He tells them that the virtues and charities, heroic acts and gathered wisdom, are nought of themselves, that the only knowledge which availeth is the Knowledge of God; and then, as if to rebuke those vain men who saw eternal life in their own act of faith, he declares that they only can find the Lord on whom the Lord looks with favour. Yet the extension of grace is linked with the exercise of our will and the beneficent use of our faculties. 'God', said Nanak, 'places salvation in good works and uprightness of conduct.'

J.D. CUNNINGHAM, *A History of the Sikhs, pp. 38–9*

Cunningham writes further about the development of the Sikh faith in the sixteenth and seventeenth centuries that:

A T THE END of the two centuries the Sikh faith had become established as a prevailing sentiment and guiding principle to work its way in the world. Nanak disengaged his little society of worshippers from Hindu idolatry and Muhammadan superstition, and placed them free on a broad basis of religious and moral purity; Amar Das preserved the infant community from declining into a sect of quietists or ascetics; Arjun gave his increasing followers a written rule of conduct and a civil organization; Har Gobind added the use of arms and a military system; and Gobind Singh bestowed upon them a distinct political existence, and inspired them with the desire of being socially free and nationally independent.

J.D. CUNNINGHAM, *A History of the Sikhs, p. 80*

F OR HISTORIANS, philologists and theologians the Adi Granth is a treasure-house which has yet to yield the full store of its riches. In the areas that concern scholars of these disciplines, its resources have been little tapped, a neglect which can be attributed to a variety of reasons. To some extent it may be an ignorance of the richness of its contents.

HEW MCLEOD, *Sikhism, p. 167*

ACCORDING TO the Sikh Gurus, God was a being to be approached and loved as a fond and faithful wife loves her spouse, and human beings to be regarded with equality as brothers, and not to be considered as divided into castes which were at variance with or despised one another.

But though the Sikhs believe in a personal God, He is not in man's image. Guru Nanak calls Him Nirankar – that is, without form. Gur Das speaks of Him as formless, without equal, wonderful, and not perceptible by the senses. At the same time all the Gurus believed that He was diffused throughout creation. Guru Nanak wrote, 'Think upon the One who is contained in everything.' This same belief was again enunciated by Guru Ram Das, 'Thou, O God, art in everything and in all places.' And, according to Guru Gobind Singh, even God and His worshipper, though two, are one, as bubbles which arise in water are again blended with it. This belief, according to the Guru, admitted of no doubt or discussion. It is the error of men in supposing distinct existence, together with the human attributes of passion and spiritual blindness, which produces sin and evil in the world and renders the soul liable to transmigration.

M.A. MACAULIFFE, *The Sikh Religion, p. lxii*

BIBLIOGRAPHY

Gurmukhi sources

Amrit Keertan (an anthology of Sikh hymns). Bazar Mai Sewan Amritsar: Khalsa Brothers, 1984

Bhai Bala, *Janam Sakhi* (stories about Guru Nanak). Bazar Mai Sewan Amritsar: Bhai Jawahar Singh Kirpal Singh & Co., n.d.

Bhai Kahn Singh Nabha, *Gur Shabad Ratnakar Mahan Kosh* (Encyclopedia of Sikh Literature), 5th edn. The Language Department Punjab, 1990 (first published 1912)

Bhai Santokh Singh, *Gur Pratap Suraj Granth (Suraj Prakash)* (writing about the Gurus and Sikhs). 1843

Giani Gian Singh, *Twarikh Guru Khalsa* (stories about Sikh Gurus and their writings). The Language Department Punjab, 1970 (first published 1893)

Sri Dasam Granth Sahib. Bazar Mai Sewan Amritsar: Bhai Chattar Singh Jiwan Singh, 1988

Sri Guru Granth Sahib. Bazar Mai Sewan Amritsar: Bhai Jawahar Singh Kirpal Singh & Co., 1965

Varan Bhai Gurdas (1551–1636) (Ballads about Sikh Gurus and Sikh living). Bazar Mai Sewan Amritsar: Bhai Chattar Singh Jiwan Singh, 1996

Other Sources

W. Owen Cole, *The Sikhs: their Religious Beliefs and Practices.* London: Routledge and Kegan Paul, 1978

W. Owen Cole with Peggy Morgan, *Six Religions in the Twentieth Century.* Amershak: Hulton Educational, 1984

J.D. Cunningham, *A History of the Sikhs: From the Origin of the Nation to the Battles of the Sutlej.* Delhi: Low Price Publications, 1990; first published 1849

Boris Klyuev, *Religion in Indian Society: The Dimensions of Unity in Diversity.* New Delhi: Sterling Publishers, 1989

C.H. Loehlin, *The Sikhs and Their Scriptures.* Lucknow: Lucknow Publishing House, 1958

M.A. McLeod, *The Sikh Religion: Its Gurus, Sacred Writings and Authors.* Oxford: Clarendon Press 1909

Hew McLeod, *Sikhism.* London: Penguin, 1997

W.H. McLeod, *Guru Nanak and the Sikh Religion.* Oxford: Clarendon Press, 1968

Peggy Morgan and Marcus Braybrooke (eds), *Testing the Global Ethic, Voices from the Religions on Moral Values.* Oxford: International Interfaith Centre/The World Congress of Faiths/CoNexus Press, 1998

Harbans Singh Doabia, *Sacred Nitnem*. Mai Sewan Amritsar: Singh Brothers, 1976

Harbans Singh Doabia, *Sacred Sukhmani*. Mai Sewan Amritsar: Singh Brothers, 1979

Manmohan Singh (trans.), *Sri Guru Granth Sahib*, 8 vols, English and Punjabi. Amritsar: Shromani Gurdwara Parbandhak, 1962

Gurbachan Singh Talib (trans.) with Bhai Jodh Singh, *Sri Guru Granth Sahib*, 3 vols, English. Patiala: Publication Bureau Punjabi University, 1987

Nikky-Gurinder Kaur Singh (trans. and ed.), *The Name of my Beloved – Verses of the Sikh Gurus*. San Fransisco: Harper Collins, 1995

Trilochan Singh *et al.* (trans.), *The Sacred Writings of the Sikhs*, revised by George S. Fraser. London: George Allen and Unwin Ltd, 1960

Susan Stronge (ed.), *The Arts of the Sikh Kingdoms*. London: V & A Publications, 1999

Paul Weller (ed.) *Religions in the UK: A Multi-Faith Directory*, 2nd edn. Derby: University of Derby, 1997